SHELLEY'S
MARY

By MARGARET LEIGHTON

The Other Island
Cleopatra: Sister of the Moon
A Hole in the Hedge
The Canyon Castaways
Voyage to Coromandel
Bride of Glory
Journey for a Princess
The Secret of Smugglers' Cove
Comanche of the Seventh
Who Rides By?

SHELLEY'S MARY

A Life of Mary Godwin Shelley

Margaret Leighton

FARRAR, STRAUS AND GIROUX   NEW YORK

To the cherished memory of my mother
Flora Kirkendall Carver

SHELLEY'S
MARY

CHAPTER ONE
1810

 The painting had hung over the mantel ever since Mary Godwin could remember and she never failed to look up at it when she entered the room. Even in the dim light of the foggiest London day, it was warm with life and color. It pictured a woman with a luminous, ardent, vivid face crowned by masses of bright auburn hair—Mary Wollstonecraft, for whom her daughter Mary was named and whose memory was revered by all the eminent visitors to the house of young Mary's father, William Godwin.

Knowing that her mother had died giving her birth had left Mary with a deep sense of regret for her own part in the tragedy. Though she had struggled to reject that instinctive guilt, carefully schooled as she had been in logic throughout her thirteen years by her renowned philosopher father, the thought continued to haunt her.

Oh, if I only could have known her! Mary had thought that at least a thousand times, looking up into the answering eyes. Her sister Fanny, four years older than Mary, had at least some precious memories of their mother. She never tired of sharing them with Mary, whom she had cherished and tried so hard to care for during the three years before William Godwin's second marriage to their widowed neighbor, Mrs. Clairmont.

The second Mrs. Godwin had soon produced a baby boy. With her own active, noisy two children, Charles and Jane Clairmont, they made up a crowded, turbulent household. Fanny had welcomed baby William, but her special love had continued to shelter and surround her own small sister. Even now, Fanny still did her best to protect pale, shy Mary from Mrs. Godwin's sharp tongue, the bullying of Charles, and Jane's mischievous teasing.

When their father had first remarried, the new Mrs. Godwin had seemed to understand and to agree with her husband's insistence that his daughters' education was of vital importance. Godwin had explained to her at length that his friend Mr. Nicholson, an expert in physiognomy, had predicted that Mary in particular would be a woman of great intelligence. He hoped she would follow in the footsteps of her wonderful mother, whose book *The Vindication of the Rights of Women* had made such an impact on the thinking of the day.

William Godwin meant to oversee the training of Mary's mind himself, as her mother would surely have done had she lived, and not send her to the usual superficial school for young ladies. He therefore had fairly crammed learning into Mary from her earliest childhood, and to his gratification, she had been a responsive pupil: she loved to read and to study and she adored her father.

When small William began to need educational guidance, however, much of his father's attention was diverted to him. Moreover, during these latter years the Godwins had embarked on a project—largely Mary's stepmother's idea—a bookshop combined with a publishing enterprise. They had moved from the suburb which was Mary's first home into a house on Skinner Street, Holborn, where their living quarters were directly over the bookshop. By this arrangement, "Mamma" could supervise the business as well as the housekeeping, and she did so with the greatest energy. Nothing escaped her gaze from behind green-tinted spectacles or her harsh, grating voice as she scolded a maidservant, a bookshop clerk, or her stepdaughter Mary, who she thought should spend more time tidying the house and less at the studies her father planned for her.

Though Mrs. Godwin revered her famous husband, she was sure of her own importance and was equally convinced that no one, not even he, appreciated the unfailing labor she put into running his house and his business. As for his constant championship of Mary Wollstonecraft's small, pale, big-eyed daughter, she resented that more and more deeply as time went on. It was clear that she believed her own Jane, almost the same age, was twice as bright and lively and attractive.

Young Mary could at least be thankful that Mrs. Godwin was not *her* mother. Her mother was Mary Wollstonecraft! Never would she forget that, not even for an instant. How often she had heard about her mother from Fanny, from her father, and from her mother's many still-devoted friends. Even as a young girl, Mary Wollstonecraft had been forced by her family's poverty to earn her own living. In a time when such a thing was almost impossible, she had educated herself enough to start a school of her own. With that experience, she had embarked upon a career of writing, first articles, then books full of new, challenging ideas on the education of girls and the place of women in the world. She had shocked and horrified many people by advocating the thorough education of girls as well as of boys and the liberation of women from their position of inferiority in society and their actual servitude to men through the laws and customs of marriage. Many others, however, forward-looking thinkers who shared William Godwin's views of social justice for all, had hailed her as a prophetess.

Mary remembered well one evening when a guest at her father's candlelit table—was it the poet Southey?—had used just that word in describing her mother. Another gentleman had then recalled admiringly how Mary Wollstonecraft had journeyed alone and unprotected to Paris in 1792. It was at the very height of French revolutionary violence, but peril had not dissuaded her. She was determined to see for herself and to report the progress of France's struggle for liberty and the rights of man against ancient, entrenched tyranny.

The discussion had barely begun when Mamma had caught sight of Mary and Fanny hovering wide-eyed in the dimness beyond the candles' glow, drinking in every word. Mamma had abruptly interrupted her guests to send the two girls off to bed and then apologized at length for their lack of manners. Her voice had clacked on and on while the company around the table glanced at one another with barely concealed annoyance. Praise of Mary Wollstonecraft was never welcomed by the second Mrs. Godwin. Even the portrait of her predecessor would have been put out of sight long ago if she had had her way.

Mary had pleasanter memories of another of their constant visitors and a great favorite of her own, Mr. Charles Lamb. His impish wit always brightened the room, delivered as it was in his odd, engaging stammer. His pranks, too. Mary almost giggled aloud whenever she recalled the occasion when he had suddenly blown out the candles on the dinner table and then, in the darkness, snatched away the cold leg of mutton which his hostess had been about to carve. He had silently deposited it on the lap of another guest and, when the candles were relit, had reproached the embarrassed man for such shocking behavior.

Mamma had been furious but she had not dared to say anything. She had even joined halfheartedly in the laughter because *Tales from Shakespeare,* written for the Godwins' publishing house by Charles Lamb and his sister, Mary, was one of their most profitable books.

Mrs. Godwin's smoldering resentment was not assuaged the next morning when her own daughter, dark-eyed, gipsyish Jane, had reenacted the scene. Jane was a clever mimic and she imitated Lamb's stutter to perfection. She did it purposely to tease her mother and succeeded so well that Mrs. Godwin at last fairly exploded with rage. Jane then went into a well-staged fainting fit which so frightened Mamma that she begged Jane's forgiveness and tried hysterically to revive her with burned feathers instead of smelling salts.

Mr. Southey was a favorite of Mary's too, because of his so often expressed admiration for her mother. Mr. Coleridge, also a poet, usually came with him, since the two had married sisters and lived together. The night he was to read aloud his *Rime of the Ancient Mariner*, Mary and Fanny concealed themselves behind a sofa and waited, crouched and breathless, while the company was at dinner. Then, just as Coleridge was about to begin his reading, Mamma's searching glance discovered them. They were hauled out and ordered harshly from the room. Only the poet's intercession saved the day for them. He could be charming when he tried and the girls were allowed to remain.

Shivers of pure delight ran along Mary's spine as the magical voice intoned the opening lines:

> "It was an ancient Mariner
> And he stoppeth one of three."

On and on he went while the room around Mary and the silent, listening faces of the others dissolved away and were gone. She was that wedding guest held by the old man's skinny hand, his glittering eye. She was aboard that doomed ship driven by storm, fog-bound in ice, or stuck day after day under a hot and coppery sky while the slain albatross hung heavily about her own neck.

"Alone, alone, all, all alone;
    Alone on a wide, wide sea."

When it was over, the room remained silent for a long time, bound by the spell of the poet's words and voice. Suddenly a sound broke the rapt hush. It was the sound of a snore—coming from Mrs. Godwin. She sat erect in her chair, her eyes hidden behind her green spectacles, but she was definitely asleep and definitely snoring. After an instant she awoke with a sudden jerk, rose, and went bustling out of the room to fetch the usual austere refreshments of tea and plain little cakes.

When she had gone, Mary saw several of the guests exchange meaningful glances, and Mr. Lamb murmured something into his neighbor's ear which set that gentleman to coughing violently in an effort to stifle his laughter.

William Godwin seemed serenely oblivious of the episode. After thanking Coleridge with Olympian condescension for his "entertaining interlude," he began a conversation which soon turned into a philosophical dissertation addressed to a group of eager lady disciples who had gathered in a reverent circle around him.

Mary wanted desperately to open her whole heart to the poet, to tell him how his reading had stirred and moved her. As so often happened to her, however, shyness choked her and no words would come. Instead, she stood gazing up at him dumbly, her grayish-hazel eyes wide in her small, heart-shaped face under its smooth cap of yellow hair.

Coleridge nodded kindly to her, then turned to Southey beside him. His remark was not meant for Mary's ears but she caught some of it: "—the cadaverous silence of the Godwin children—to me quite catacombish," he said.

Mary could not hear Southey's answer, but she saw both men turn as one and look earnestly and sadly up at the portrait over the mantel.

CHAPTER TWO
1810–1814

The London weather continued to be sunless and raw all through the autumn of 1810. In the house on Skinner Street the chilly gloom was deepened by the fact that Godwin and Company's bookshop was running into financial difficulties. Godwin managed to avoid most confrontations with business problems by shutting himself up in his study to write. When things got too desperate, he would go so far as to send eloquent and persuasive letters to affluent friends, thereby extracting loans which he never found himself able to repay. He was glad to leave all other details to his formidable wife, for he chose to believe her claims to shrewdness and executive ability and remained blind to the fact that her truculent quarreling with employees and even with customers brought on most of their difficulties.

His daughter Mary, however, could find no place of refuge from Mamma's incessantly clacking voice. She suffered fits of trembling and one morning awoke to find a numbness in one of her arms. By spring she could not make it function properly and a doctor was summoned.

"A form of nervous paralysis," he stated, and recommended a complete change of scene.

When the doctor had gone, William Godwin shook his head in bewilderment. How could he afford to provide a change of scene for Mary? But something must be managed, of course.

Mrs. Godwin, as always, had an opinion ready. She reminded her husband that one of his many admiring lady disciples lived by the seashore at Ramsgate. Surely something could be suggested to her? Letters were thereupon exchanged and arrangements made. In May, Mamma, Mary, Charles, Jane, and William traveled to the seaside, leaving Fanny to keep house for their father. After a few weeks' holiday, the three other children and their mother returned to London while Mary stayed on under the care of the accommodating Miss Petman.

The change Mary needed had been not so much of air as of company, and not until the others had gone home did she begin to feel the benefit of her release. Her tension relaxed. The numbness in her arm vanished. She walked the firm sands of the beach every morning, breathing in the salt-laden air, watching the gulls swoop and dive in the frothy breakers and the sails of the fishing fleet fade away toward the horizon and the misty shores of France. Beyond those shores, she knew, Bonaparte still hung like a menacing thundercloud over Europe. English armies were among those confronting him there, although Nelson's famous victory at Trafalgar, six years before, had halted his threat to invade England.

Miss Petman had a fair-sized and varied library, and Mary now spent happy hours reading there, uninterrupted by the noisy, quarreling Clairmonts or Mamma's scolding. A nearby bay was famous for its shrimps, and Mary feasted on them. Her pallor gave way to a rosy-golden tan and her cheeks rounded out. "Why, you're almost pretty, my dear!" Miss Petman exclaimed with a surprise that was scarcely flattering.

Mary stayed at Ramsgate until December, then returned to the house on Skinner Street with mixed feelings. She was genuinely eager to rejoin her adored father and Fanny, but the prospect of a reunion with the others filled her with a dread she could not reason away. It did not help matters when, on Mary's first evening at home, Jane put on one of her well-staged tantrums. Her mother had asked her to do some minor chore of housekeeping, and Jane refused haughtily on the ground that she must practice and perfect her French accent and do it in the privacy of her room.

In the dispute that ensued, Mrs. Godwin's scolding resounded through the house with all the familiar clangor, punctuated by Jane's shrill, screamed replies. Ten-year-old William at once joined in, howling out some grievance of his own, while Fanny rushed from one to the other in a vain effort to keep the peace.

As the weeks moved on, Mary's color faded, she lost weight again and drooped visibly. Fanny worried over her, and more than once Mary saw her father's eyes rest on her with a vague concern. He was engrossed in his writing, however, and also in his son's education. Young William was a bright, promising student and already he was being taken along with the others to the theater and to lectures.

One of the educational tasks which William Godwin set for his children was the presentation of talks from time to time on subjects he chose for them. A workman in the shop had built a miniature pulpit and set it up in the living room. On February 15, 1812, a group of invited guests were privileged to hear small William deliver a lecture from this pulpit. His father had selected the theme and Mary had written the lecture, which was entitled "The Influence of Government on the Character of the People."

Among the company that evening was a gentleman with pleasant, easy manners, from faraway America. His name was Aaron Burr and in his journal he recorded that William spoke "with gravity and decorum." The Godwin young people had been told only that Burr was a former Vice-President of the United States, but Jane found out— and whispered the news to Mary—that Aaron Burr had killed a man named Alexander Hamilton in a famous duel. Later he had been tried in a high court for another crime, that of conspiracy to commit treason. He had been acquitted, but ever since then he had been living in exile, far from his native land. Jane was thrilled to be in the same room with a man she thought so dangerous.

Mary tried not to stare too openly at Burr's worn, once-handsome face as she passed him the simple little cakes Mrs. Godwin supplied for her guests' refreshment. He took one and then, to her surprise, thanked her by name and added a few words of praise for her composition of the lecture they had just heard.

"Whatever did he say to you?" Jane demanded as soon as they were alone together in the serving pantry.

When Mary repeated his compliment, Jane tossed her head and hurried off to her mother. A moment later Mrs. Godwin clapped her hands for attention and announced that Jane would sing some songs for the guests. Jane's voice was true and pleasing and she sang very well. She had chosen some old Irish airs lately made popular by the new words written for them by the famous poet Tom Moore. The guests were plainly enchanted and Jane glowed with pleasure at their applause. After that Mr. Lamb called for a dance from all of the girls, and in this, too, Jane was the star performer. Eyes sparkling, cheeks scarlet, she twirled and spun through the figures, light-footed as a gypsy. She looked a little crestfallen, however, when she saw Mr. Burr murmur some polite excuse to his host and slip away before her dance had ended.

February dragged on, then March and April. The Godwin household's bickering continued, constantly exploding into noisy quarrels. Mary found herself always drawn into them somehow, but whichever side she chose was considered wrong by Mamma until even in Mary's dreams that harsh voice came rasping through. Her weakness and trembling returned until at last her father could ignore them no longer.

This time he turned to another admirer, a well-to-do businessman of Dundee, Scotland, named Baxter. Godwin

wrote him of his problem with Mary's health, and Baxter
and his wife were soon persuaded to take Mary into their
home with the provision that their two daughters, Christie
and Isabella, would be welcome to stay with the Godwins
whenever they visited London.

On June 7, 1812, Mary set sail on the ship *Osburgh* for
Dundee. Much as she longed to escape from the intolerable atmosphere at home, she was essentially shy, dependent, and timid, and the prospect of this voyage to be
taken alone suddenly terrified her. Even on short excursions by water from Ramsgate, the motion of the waves
had made her dizzy and ill, and this trip might last as
much as a week. She clung to her father in tears until he
had to speak sternly to her in order to extricate himself.

The ordeal by sea was even worse than Mary had feared.
She arrived at Dundee so racked and exhausted by seasickness that she could barely stand. "You poor wee lassie!"
Mrs. Baxter exclaimed at the sight of her, and took her into
her motherly arms.

The Baxter household was hard-working and busy, but
it was also cheerful, and above all it was affectionate.
Christie and Isabella set about at once to restore Mary to
health by taking her with them on walks among the
heathery hills and on picnics in the hayfields. Mrs. Baxter
pressed food upon her at every meal. "You'll soon have
cheeks as round and rosy as these Scottish girls of mine,"
she promised.

Mary's fair, almost milk-white skin never attained the
high-colored brilliance of the Baxter girls' complexion, but

during the long northern-summer days she revived and bloomed under their delighted eyes. A friendship that was to last for years sprang up between Mary and Isabella, while Christie, older than the two, was always kind and understanding. Although they did not share Mary's habit of serious study, they respected her need for peaceful, un-interrupted hours. One of her greatest pleasures was to set off alone with her books to some solitary, sunlit hillside overlooking the Firth of Tay to read awhile and then to launch out into long daydreams of the future. In these dreams Mary saw herself fulfilling her father's hopes, by some miracle throwing off her shyness and becoming as brave and independent as Mary Wollstonecraft had been. She was happy and relaxed, and her nights were filled with untroubled sleep.

Fanny wrote faithfully but her well-meant letters always disturbed Mary's tenuous, new-found security. Papa was still writing busily, Fanny told her. Mamma had dismissed one of the men who worked in the shop and hired another, but he seemed as lazy and inefficient as the first. Jane was teasing to be sent to a fashionable boarding school, but where was the tuition to come from? Especially when one of the gentlemen from whom Papa was long accustomed to borrow was being selfish and unkind about further loans? Fanny was glad, nevertheless, that Mary was enjoying herself so much, away from all the worries that vexed the rest of her family.

At harvest time the Baxter girls and Mary made a holiday of helping in the grain fields, gathering and binding the dusty golden sheaves. Then, in late autumn, Christie decided to visit London and take Mary along to see her family.

Mary's feeling was less eagerness than apprehension, but there was comfort in the knowledge that the visit would be brief and that she would be returning with Christie. The southward voyage was smooth, for a wonder, and Mary was only slightly seasick—another fact which gave her strength to face the coming ordeal.

They found things on Skinner Street in their usual turbulent state, but, to Mary's heartfelt relief, Christie's presence served to moderate Mamma's voice somewhat. During their stay a young poet, Percy Bysshe Shelley, and his wife came to dinner. Shelley was a tall, loose-jointed young man with unruly fair hair and vivid blue eyes, his wife pretty as a picture in a modish purple satin gown.

Mrs. Godwin paid them both marked attention, and Christie spoke afterward of the elegance of the lady and of what an intelligent conversationalist Mr. Shelley was for one barely twenty years old.

Shelley was one of Godwin's most ardent disciples, it seemed, and, what Mrs. Godwin thought more interesting, was heir to a baronetcy and a great fortune—an income of six thousand pounds a year! Mamma found Shelley a welcome change from the penniless poets and writers who came to the house only for a good meal.

When Mary returned to Scotland soon afterward, she carried with her a lingering memory of Shelley's eager, rapid voice, and the blue of his eyes stayed oddly clear in her mind. Once again the Baxters' affection enfolded her. Sheltered and surrounded by praise and love, during the two years that followed she blossomed visibly from a shy, thin, nervous child into a girl poised eagerly on the verge of womanhood. A very pretty girl, Isabella Baxter often assured her, although Mary could not quite believe her. Her mother's portrait remained her standard of beauty. Compared with that opulent, glowing loveliness, Mary's own gray eyes, white skin, and fine golden-yellow hair seemed pale indeed.

Fanny's letters still arrived regularly, but they no longer had the power to shake Mary's new-won serenity. Mamma was just the same, Fanny wrote. Jane had finally succeeded in her demand and was at a boarding school kept by a cultured French lady. Jane could now jabber in French like a native, or so she maintained. William was also in school, and Charles was working in Edinburgh.

The main theme of Fanny's letters now seemed to be Mr. Shelley. That extraordinary young man had proved to be the benefactor they had needed for so long. He had promised to pay all of Papa's debts! It was truly a miracle, for Papa's creditors were becoming more and more disagreeable. One was even threatening to have him put in debtors' prison. "Mr. Shelley is so kind, even to me," Fanny added in closing. "He talks with me, writes me long letters, and is directing and advising me in my reading."

As Mary watched the spring of 1814 approach, she looked forward with quiet pleasure to another summer of long, happy days in the open air. Her own world, like the great one about her, seemed bright and promising. The Allies had won a series of victories over Bonaparte, the ogre who had menaced Europe and England ever since Mary could remember. With him gone there would surely be peace at last! Peace! Might not peace bring to England too a chance for the social reforms which the French Revolution had begun so gloriously and which her father and mother had both advocated so long and so vainly? Perhaps she would have a part in bringing those about, Mary told herself. Mary Wollstonecraft Godwin was a great name— if only she could live up to it! And she turned with new energy to her studies.

In May a letter from her father shattered her plans. She must return home now that she had regained her health, he wrote. She was already sixteen and he had not educated her for a life of idle pleasure. It was high time for her to make herself useful in the house and the shop and help her overburdened Mamma, especially since Fanny would soon be leaving to aid her Wollstonecraft aunts in their school in Dublin.

Once again Mary went aboard a ship bound for London, but this time she was without the comforting hope of returning. Saying goodbye to the kind Baxters was almost more than she could bear, and the tears came. Fanny and Papa, Papa and Fanny—she loved them both and would be happy to see them. But Mamma and the Clairmonts!

The household on Skinner Street seemed to her to be in even worse turmoil than she had feared. On the very day Mary arrived, Jane locked herself in her room with a threat of suicide, and her hysterical shrieks rang out above the pleas her mother shouted through the door. The cause of it all, Fanny explained, was Jane's decision to become an actress—a career which Mamma abhorred and absolutely forbade. Young William seemed more obnoxiously spoiled than ever, while Charles, still in Edinburgh, wrote long, whining letters about his unhappy state there and begged to be allowed to come home.

Mamma's temper was worse than ever, Fanny told Mary, especially because Shelley had delayed in getting the money he had promised to Godwin. Shelley was just frittering away his time, traveling back and forth to Ireland and around the country on harebrained projects for aiding the working classes, claimed Mrs. Godwin, and though of course she was sorry for them, her husband's welfare was much more important to the world. But Fanny felt sure that Shelley was doing his best. At last he was back in London and promised to have twelve hundred pounds of the three thousand Godwin needed by the sixth of July.

Though Mary had met him only once, it was strange how clear her recollection of Shelley was. He had remembered her too, he told Mary when he arrived next for dinner. When his wife was away he dined with the Godwins almost every day. How could he forget one of Mary Wollstonecraft's daughters? He sent a reverent glance up at the portrait as he spoke. He had changed in some way, Mary thought. His face was thinner—even a little haggard, she noted with a pang—and his expensively tailored clothes looked rumpled, neglected, and unbrushed.

His blue eyes were as full of light as ever, his voice as boyishly eager. His discussions with her father ranged widely over philosophical topics. He had first read Godwin's *Political Justice* when he was at school at Eton, Mary learned, and from that moment it had become the guiding beacon of his life. His enthusiasm for its teachings had led him to write his pamphlet *The Necessity for Atheism,* which had caused his expulsion from Oxford. It had also brought his father's wrath down upon him as well as much harassment and even persecution from government and Church authorities. He had held to those ideals steadily, nevertheless, with the proud certainty that their truth would ultimately prevail and would lead the world one day to "happy regions of eternal hope"—words which he quoted from his own privately printed philosophical poem *Queen Mab.*

Mary listened, wholly entranced. There was fire and excitement in his every phrase and glance, yet an indescribable sweetness and kindness too. When dinner was over and the men retired to the study, she evaded Mamma and followed, spellbound, to sit in a shadowy corner and drink in Shelley's voice and his words. Whenever their eyes met, as they did more and more often, something terrifying and at the same time thrilling stabbed through her body.

Each evening that he was there it was the same. At last Mamma sensed that something was growing between them and she intervened by sending Mary off to her room.

First it was Fanny mooning about and making a fool of herself over him—that's why she was being sent off to Dublin—and now Mary!

Mary's household tasks allowed her a few hours' leisure in the afternoon, and since she was banished from the discussions in the study, she sought a haven where she could read and dream undisturbed. Mary Wollstonecraft's grave was in St. Pancras' Cemetery. Whenever her daughter could steal away, she took refuge there with her books, finding comfort in the cool green shade and in the sense of nearness to her mother's spirit. Because Shelley had praised them, the two volumes she always brought with her were *The Vindication of the Rights of Women* by her mother and her father's *Political Justice*. She read the familiar pages over and over until she knew them almost by heart.

Then one day a miracle happened. Shelley himself came walking toward her along a path through the sun-dappled shade like some bright-haired apparition from another world. He had been guided there by—of all people—Jane! "Mr. Shelley kept asking where you were, why he never saw you any more, so I brought him here," Jane explained. Her smile was mischievous and meaningful as she departed with an airy wave of her hand.

For a moment neither of them spoke. Then Shelley stooped and picked up one of her books. "What is this? Ah, your father's *Political Justice*, of course." He sat down cross-legged on the short grass beside her, opened the volume, and leafed through the pages. "Here is a passage I've found of great significance and value." He began to read it aloud to her.

So started weeks of secret meetings in which they read together from the books he brought. Soon they began to pour out their thoughts and hopes to each other. Mary told of her deep love for her father and her misery under Mrs. Godwin's domination. He had sensed that situation from the beginning of their acquaintance, he said. He shared her opinion of Godwin's wife and longed to help Mary in any way he could. He understood her feelings only too well, for he had suffered in much the same way. His own father was a tyrant who had made every effort to shackle his freedom of thought and action. Shelley had broken away from parental bondage at last, but the struggle had cost him great anguish, for now he was forbidden to visit his childhood home or to see his mother and sisters, whom he dearly loved.

His grandfather, old Sir Bysshe Shelley, the baronet, was one of those curses upon society who had amassed great wealth at the expense of the poor, Shelley explained to Mary on another day. His father, Timothy Shelley of Field Place, was a typically bigoted country squire, filled with all the overweening pride of his class, who thought only of his own selfish pleasures. Because his eldest son had openly espoused the cause of the suffering poor against their exploitation by both Church and state, Timothy had pared down his allowance to a pittance and would have cut him off entirely as his heir if the property were not entailed to him by law. Of course the law of entail was an outdated evil which must be abolished, Shelley stated dogmatically, but since he planned to do nothing but good with the money when it was his, he was willing to receive it as a sort of trust.

Now even Harriet, his wife, had turned against him and the high principles which she once had seemed to share. He had eloped with her from her school and married her solely out of chivalry—not for love, he said—to save her from the cruelty of her family and the abuse of her teachers and schoolmates. Now she had lost all interest in the poetry and philosophy which were necessary to his very life. She had cruelly refused to nurse their child, Ianthe, and instead had hired a wet nurse. Harriet wished to be set up as a lady of quality with a coach of her own, silver plate, and expensive gowns, Shelley said. When he objected, for the world of fashion was abhorrent to him, she had flounced off to Bath, where, according to rumor, she was engaged in a flirtation with a dissolute army officer.

This was perhaps the final blow, he declared. His face darkened as he showed Mary a small vial of laudanum. "I carry this with me always," he said. "There may come a time when this will be the only possible solution to the problems that beset my life."

At this Mary gasped, "No! No! No!" The next instant they were in each other's arms.

CHAPTER THREE
1814

 June passed and July approached. Mary went about the house in a daze of bewildered bliss, barely conscious of what was happening around her, living only from one secret tryst in the churchyard to the next. Could it be possible that this glorious being loved *her* more than anyone else in the world? She hardly awakened from her trance enough to say goodbye when Fanny left for Dublin. Fanny knew nothing of the lovers' meetings, but she had felt some great change in both Shelley and her sister from the time they had met. The sad, reproachful look she gave Mary as they parted would have troubled the younger girl if she had not been so entirely wrapped up in her own happiness.

They must be united, Shelley stated passionately, and he promised to clear away every obstacle that kept them apart. He would explain it all to Harriet and would make generous provision for her and their child. He had always maintained that the wedding ceremony was the merest empty formality—without true love, marriage simply did not exist—and he was positive that Harriet shared that view. As for Mary's father, Godwin in his writings had advocated the complete freedom of love without marriage. He had, in fact, described marriage as the most inexcusable of monopolies. Could he logically object if his daughter followed those teachings and joined her life to Shelley's?

Shelley had presented Mary with a copy of his *Queen Mab,* in which he had expressed much of his radical philosophy, and Mary poured out her feeling for him on the blank pages in the back of the volume.

"July, 1814. This book is sacred to me, and as no other creature shall ever look into it, I may write in it what I please—yet what shall I write?—that I love the author beyond all powers of expression and that I am parted from him, dearest and only love—by that love we have promised each other, although I may not be yours, I can never be another's. But I am thine, exclusively thine,

> By the kiss of love, the glance none saw beside
> The smile none else might understand
> The whispered thoughts of hearts allied
> The pressure of the thrilling hand.

"I have pledged myself to thee, and sacred is the gift. I remember your words: 'You are now, Mary, going to mix with many, and for the moment I shall depart, but in the solitude of your chamber I shall be with you.' Yes, you are ever with me, sacred vision.

> But ah! I feel in this was given
> A blessing never meant for me,
> Thou art too like a dream from heaven
> For earthly love to merit thee!"

The departure Shelley had mentioned to her was for the purpose of raising the twelve hundred pounds he had promised to deliver to Godwin. At last, on July 6, he arrived at Skinner Street bearing the long-awaited sum in the form of a draft on his bankers. Shelley handed it to Godwin; then, in a sudden outpouring of words, he confessed his love for Mary and asked her father's permission to take her away with him as soon as he could make suitable arrangements with Harriet, his wife.

To Shelley's astonishment, the philosopher of liberalism and free love exploded in shocked wrath. He shook his finger in the young man's face as he thundered his refusal. Shelley must banish such a licentious project from his mind forever. He must return to his lawful wife and his child at once. At the same time, however, Godwin continued to hold tightly to the bank draft which Shelley had just given him.

Pale and shaken, Shelley rushed from the house while Mary fled sobbing to her room. With Shelley gone, her parents' anger turned upon Mary. This was all her fault, both told her. It was no more than a silly, girlish infatuation, Godwin added sternly. It would soon pass, and in the meantime he forbade her to see or communicate with Shelley.

Mamma was blunter. How dared the girl imperil her father's prospects by brazenly throwing herself at Shelley just as he was beginning to be of some solid financial help to them all?

Mary was confined to her room, but Jane told her, a

few days later, that Harriet Shelley had arrived in London, summoned by a letter from her husband. She had called in great distress upon the Godwins, weeping the whole time and vowing that she still loved Shelley devotedly. The Godwins promised not to allow Shelley to come to the house any more.

When Jane reported this to the grieving Mary, the two decided to slip out of the house and go to see Harriet Shelley themselves. Mary's heart pounded so violently that she could hardly get her breath as Harriet received them in the inn parlor. Then, before Mary could speak, Harriet launched into a passionate tirade. From her position as a blameless, injured wife she denounced the white-faced, trembling Mary as a seductress.

Before the meeting Mary had marshaled her arguments with care, but now, in the face of Harriet's indignant tears, her words sounded weak and false even to herself. She got no help from Jane, who sat, bright-eyed with pleased excitement, glancing from one speaker to the other as though she were watching a play.

When Harriet paused for an instant, Mary ventured, "But since we both love him so much, would it not be possible for us all three to live together, I as his sister, you as his wife?"

Harriet got up as though lifted bodily by outraged virtue. "Did Bysshe suggest that to you? It sounds like one of his fantastic notions. Never, never would I consent to such a heathenish arrangement, nor would any other respectable Englishwoman. I am his lawful wife, the mother of his child and of another soon to be born. If you are not utterly depraved you will promise me here and now to give him up."

Another child soon to be born? *His* child! This news was so unexpected that it was like a body blow. Mary burst into tears. Stammering out her promise, she hurried away.

A few days later Mary was in the schoolroom trying with small success to focus her mind on a Latin translation when she heard a confusion of voices in the shop below. Hurried steps mounted the stairs and with them the sound of Mamma's voice raised in angry protest. The door flew open and Shelley appeared, Mrs. Godwin close behind him, with Jane at her heels.

Shelley's face was ghastly, his eyes glittering as if with fever. "They wish to separate us, my beloved," he cried, his voice cracked and hoarse. "But this shall unite us." He held a vial of laudanum out to her and she took it automatically, then stared down at it in horror. "By this you can escape from tyranny and this shall reunite me to you." He drew a small pistol from his pocket and held it up for her to see.

Such cold terror gripped Mary that she could neither move nor speak. Jane began to shriek hysterically, but for once Mrs. Godwin paid her no attention. "Your father is out, but Marshall is working in the study. I'll fetch him," she said, and ran from the room.

Mary found her voice at last: it was only a whisper. "No, not that! We'll find some other way—there must be another way. I promise to be ever faithful to you, no matter what happens, if you will only calm yourself, my darling!"

Slowly he relaxed and lowered the pistol. By the time Marshall ventured into the room, pushed from behind by Mrs. Godwin, Shelley had put the pistol in his pocket. He gave Mary a long, earnest look, and stumbled out the door. They heard his feet on the stairs and then the sound of the shop door as it slammed behind him.

Mary lived through the next days and nights like a sleepwalker, barely hearing her father's stern lectures or Mamma's furious ranting. More than once loneliness and grief brought her to the point where she regretted having refused Shelley's desperate remedy. How was she to endure the bleak emptiness she now saw stretching before her after the dazzling radiance that Shelley's love had brought into her life?

About a week after Shelley's wild visit, the doorbell of the Skinner Street house clanged loudly at midnight. Godwin hurried down to find Shelley's landlord with the message that Shelley had taken laudanum. Godwin and his wife hurried to Shelley's lodgings.

When they arrived, they found that the doctor had got Shelley to his feet and was forcing him to walk up and down the room. But he was still in grave danger. Mrs. Godwin was an able nurse and also a determined woman. She stayed with him, caring for him, all the next day, for it was unthinkable to her that this prime source of financial aid should disappear from their horizon. Godwin meanwhile sent for one of Shelley's most devoted older friends, Mrs.

de Boinville of Bracknell, who took over the task until the young man at last recovered.

When Shelley was up and about again, Mary managed, with Jane's help, to slip away for another meeting with him in the churchyard—a "last meeting before they must part forever!" One glimpse of his ravaged face swept away all her resolution, even her promise to Harriet, and she was in his arms again.

He had already formed a plan for them to escape together, he told her as he held her close. He had arranged with his bankers for Harriet's support. Harriet could draw as she wished from his account and so would be amply provided for. As for Mary's father, once they were gone Godwin would surely realize that they were only following his own teachings and he would be reconciled with them.

"I'll have a post chaise waiting at the corner of Hatton Garden before dawn on July twenty-eighth," he said. "You must leave the house quietly and join me there. We'll drive to Dover, then cross to France and travel on to Switzerland, where unimagined joy and bliss await us, free and together at last."

When Mary hesitated, frightened and appalled by so bold a venture, Jane assured her that she would help manage the escape.

And so it was arranged. Before even the earliest light of summer dawn, the two girls glided silently down the stairs in their stockinged feet and out the door, paused to put on their shoes, then hurried through the empty streets. They wore their black silk Sunday dresses and carried only one small portmanteau. "Mamma would notice if we packed anything more," said Jane, who had taken charge of the process. "Besides, Shelley will buy you all the clothes you wish, once you reach Paris. What fun that will be!"

Shelley was pacing nervously beside the dim shape of the carriage, his watch in his hand. After his swift, welcoming embrace Mary turned to say goodbye to Jane and saw to her surprise that her stepsister had climbed into the carriage. "I daren't return to face Mamma," Jane explained, settling herself back in the seat with a high-pitched giggle. "I'll have to come with you."

"Get in quickly, Mary darling," Shelley urged when she faltered, confused by this new turn of events. "There's no time to lose." Mary obeyed, Shelley swung aboard, the driver cracked his whip, the horses plunged forward with a clatter of hoofs, and they were off through the warm summer darkness toward Dover.

When the sun rose through heavy thunderclouds, the warmth increased. Combined with the rocking motion of the coach, the heat began to affect Mary with something very like seasickness. At every stage stop for fresh horses they had to linger awhile for her to rest and recover, until Shelley, fearing that the Godwins might be pursuing them, hired four horses instead of two to carry them on faster. They reached Dover at four in the afternoon, and there Mary was able at last to refresh herself by a dip in the sea.

The next packet boat for Calais did not leave until the following morning, they learned. "We daren't wait for that," Shelley exclaimed. After some bargaining he hired a couple of sailors to take them across the Channel in their boat, a light fishing smack.

Mary described that voyage in her journal. "The evening was most beautiful . . . there was but little wind, and the sails flapped in the sagging breeze; the moon rose and night came on and with the night a slow, heavy swell and a fresh breeze, which soon produced a sea so violent as to toss the boat very much. I was dreadfully sea-sick and as is usually my custom when thus affected, I slept during the greater part of the night, awakening only from time to time to ask where we were, and to receive the dismal answer each time, 'Not quite half way.'

"The wind was violent and contrary; if we could not reach Calais the sailors proposed making for Boulogne. They promised only two hours' sail from shore, yet hour after hour passed, and we were still far distant when the moon sank on the red and stormy horizon and the fast-flashing lightning became pale in the breaking day.

"We were proceeding slowly against the wind when suddenly a thunder squall struck the sail, and the waves rushed into the boat; even the sailors acknowledged that our situation was perilous; but they succeeded in reefing the sail; the wind was now changed, and we drove before the gale directly to Calais."

Jane had been frightened and subdued during the voyage, but Shelley was in the highest of spirits. He loved the sea, and danger only stimulated him. Once they were on dry land Mary's seasickness vanished, and she gazed about her with delight and wonder. "Look, Mary, the sun rises over France," Shelley said.

France! The country her mother had known so well! Mary's spirits soared to meet Shelley's. Safe and secure at last in his love, everything delighted her—the quaint old fortified town, the language and dress and manners of the people, the neat, polite servants at Dessein's Hotel, where they engaged rooms and ordered dinner. Some of Shelley's luggage had had to be left behind at Dover because of the smallness of their boat; it was to be brought over that evening by packet. They would have to wait for it before going on to Paris.

They were laughing and talking over a fine dinner at the hotel when an Englishman approached their table. He introduced himself to Shelley as Captain Davidson and said that he had just arrived on the Dover packet. "There's a fat lady just come ashore from our vessel. She says that Mr. Shelley has run off with her daughter," he announced, looking vastly amused.

"Mamma!" Jane exclaimed. Mary turned so pale that Shelley feared she was going to faint. "Go and deal with her, Jane, and keep her away from Mary," he urged.

For the first time, then, Mary and Shelley were alone together. They were only beginning to taste that pleasure when Jane rejoined them with the news that she had refused to return with her mother to the prison of Skinner Street and had cast her lot with them and with liberty!

Jane sounded so triumphantly happy that for a moment

Mary could not bring herself to protest. Shelley, however, looked startled and sober. "But, my dear girl, this is too important a step for you to take lightly," he said. "You must consider it with more care. The packet won't return to Dover for several hours. Use that time to give the matter your gravest thought."

Jane sat down in her chair, folded her hands in her lap, and drew her brows together in a frown that was plainly an attempt at the most serious pondering. In a very short time she jumped to her feet and tripped off to give her decision to her mother. She did it with brutal frankness. The dull, cramped poverty of Skinner Street was not for her, she said. She belonged rather to this larger world of adventure, of travel in foreign lands. Mrs. Godwin was too exhausted by the ordeal of her long pursuit to have anything to say in reply. She left alone on the Dover packet and Jane returned once again to Mary and Shelley.

The small cloud of Jane's presence was not enough to shadow Mary's bliss, now that Mamma had gone and she knew that she was actually safe from her stepmother's clutches forever. Shelley was at his merriest as he and Mary strolled the cobbled streets, arm in arm. Lightheaded with relief, Mary found herself laughing aloud like a pleased child at everything she saw in the town. Then they returned to the hotel through the sea-scented dusk to share their first night of joyous love.

CHAPTER FOUR
1814–1815

About six o'clock in the evening of July 30, they set off in a hired cabriolet for Paris. The vehicle was "drawn by three horses, the tallest in the middle," Mary wrote in her journal; the driver, "a queer little fellow with a long pig-tail." Their first stop was at Boulogne, where they had planned only to rest. They were all so tired, however, that they spent the night there, then went on the next day as far as Abbeville. After that they traveled both day and night without rest until they reached Paris on Tuesday, August 2.

Lodged in rooms at the Hôtel de Vienne, the three were full of eager plans. First they would call on Mary Wollstonecraft's friend Helen Williams. Then, of course, they would view the sights of the great city—the city now liberated from the clutches of Napoleon Bonaparte by the victorious Allies. The defeated Emperor had abdicated earlier in the spring and had gone to live in exile on the island of Elba. For this deliverance all of Europe and England too had sent up prayers of thanksgiving.

Both Shelley and Mary planned to continue their reading and study during this journey; most of Shelley's luggage consisted of books and manuscripts he had brought along to work on. Shelley expected also to draw funds from a man named Tavernier, the Paris correspondent of his London business agent, Hookham. This was essential, for he had spent his money so lavishly during their travels that he had almost none left.

They set off blithely through the city to call upon Miss Williams, only to learn that she was out of town. M. Tavernier was available, but he proved to be far too prudent to honor Shelley's draft without confirmation from Hookham. The knowledge that they were almost penniless in a foreign city might have dampened their gaiety if Shelley had not gone out and sold his handsome gold watch and chain for enough to tide them over until Hookham's letter should arrive.

They could not do the shopping for clothes which Jane had expected, but they continued with their sightseeing as lightheartedly as ever. Jane's fluency in French was proving an asset, and Shelley remarked in private to Mary that Jane was too nice a girl to be left to the care of Mrs. Godwin—"such a vulgar, commonplace woman, without an idea of philosophy; I do not think her a proper person to form the mind of a young girl." He himself would be pleased to assume that duty, he promised.

They passed a radiantly happy week, scarcely aware of the hot, oppressive August weather. Then the letter from Hookham arrived and Tavernier advanced the sum of sixty pounds to Shelley. After much discussion they de-

cided to travel from Paris to Switzerland on foot. Not only
would this be economical, they agreed, but actual contact
with the earth of France would give them a far better feeling for the natural beauties of the region than whirling
through them in a coach.

Their plan was regarded as utter madness by the pro-
prietress of their hotel, who had taken a motherly interest
in the young trio. She warned them of the hardships and
even dangers they were sure to meet in a countryside so
recently swept over by battling armies. "Ex-soldiers who
are no better than brigands are still roaming the roads.
They are periling all foot travelers. As for young girls—"
She rolled her eyes in horror.

They were not to be deterred, however. Shelley went
out early in the morning to the animal market to purchase
a donkey, which was to carry their luggage and upon
which his fragile and cherished Mary could ride whenever
she should tire. He returned with a beast that seemed un-
believably small and weak even to her unpracticed eyes. "It
looked so unhappy there in the market," Shelley explained
earnestly. "It almost spoke aloud its desire to belong to
someone who would treat it kindly. With good care and
food it will soon be a different animal."

Unfortunately, when they tried to load their possessions
on the donkey, the creature's head began to droop lower
and lower, it started to tremble, and, in spite of Shelley's
frantic efforts to hold it up, its hind legs slowly gave way
and collapsed under it until it was practically sitting on
the ground. They removed the burdens and got it to its

feet somehow, but even then it could barely totter along the road.

During the last few miles before they reached the town of Charenton, Shelley had to support the beast by main strength while the two girls trailed behind in their black silk dresses, carrying the luggage by turns. At Charenton they exchanged the donkey and some additional money for a sturdy mule and continued on their way. Far from being discouraged, the three young travelers found their misadventures so novel and amusing that they had to pause as often to laugh as to rest. Even the many discomforts of the country inns where they lodged were only fresh subjects for Shelley's puckish humor.

On the fourth day of their foot travel Shelley strained a muscle in his leg, with the result that he, not Mary, had to ride the mule into the city of Troyes. While they waited there for Shelley's leg to heal, he busied himself in writing letters to friends in England, among them his wife, Harriet. He had not forgotten her, he assured her. He was still her "firm and constant friend." Switzerland was their destination, and he urged her to make ready to join them there in "some sweet retreat I shall procure for you among the mountains." He described their travels in detail, including the ravages left by the war, and ended by sending his love to their child, "my sweet little Ianthe." He signed it "ever most affectionately yours."

When he read the letter aloud for Mary's approval, she remembered Harriet's indignant reaction to her own suggestion that they all live together. But when she expressed these misgivings to Shelley, he assured her with the utmost confidence that by this time Harriet would have thought things over more reasonably and would understand and appreciate the generosity of his offer. He was so positive that he was right and so eloquent in expressing himself that all of Mary's doubts were swept away.

Besides writing letters, Shelley began, in the inn at Troyes, to outline another of his long, philosophical poems, while Mary, at his urging, continued to work on a novel she had begun at home. Entitled *Hate,* it was a somber book concerned with the way in which evil passions engender evil deeds.

Shelley's leg was still giving him trouble, and so, to prevent further delay, he bought an open carriage and engaged a driver to take them the rest of the way to Neuchâtel in Switzerland. The driver proved to be a gruff, impatient fellow. He had been delighted at first to be hired by one of the "English milords," for they were reputed to be lavish and generous patrons. He was soon baffled and disgruntled, however, by his passengers' erratic manner of travel. They were constantly stopping him so that they might get out and admire the view or to picnic on a modest meal of bread and cheese and fruit in some pleasant spot. Worst of all, they put up at the cheapest of inns and seemed entirely uninterested in the hearty food and drink he had counted upon.

Once when the three young people had paused to explore a thick pine forest, he shouted several times to recall them, then whipped up his horses and drove off in a huff, leaving them all behind. They were forced to walk to the nearest town and hire a boy to ride after him, then to hire another carriage before they finally caught up with him and their baggage at Pontarlier on August 19.

They crossed the border into Switzerland at St. Sulpice, more than ever enraptured as the mountain scenery began to open before them. In Neuchâtel they halted again to pick up some money Shelley's friend Thomas Love Peacock had sent him by way of a local banker—not nearly as much as Shelley had expected, he complained. In order to "make it go farther," he obtained it all in silver and returned to the inn staggering under the weight of the canvas bag that held the coins.

Shelley hired another carriage and driver to carry them to Lucerne, and from there they took a boat down the lake of Lucerne to Brunnen. They quartered themselves at first in a romantic-looking, half-ruined castle made over into an inn; although picturesque, this proved thoroughly uncomfortable. Shelley then took a fancy to another lodging called "The Château" and impulsively leased it for the next six months.

Here they settled down at last, resolved to enjoy what they termed their "earthly paradise beside the mountain-shadowed lake." That evening Shelley unpacked his books and read aloud to the two girls from Tacitus, the Abbé Barruel, and Shakespeare. He also worked on his new poem, in which he now incorporated vivid descriptions of the Alpine scenery all around them. Mary too worked on her novel, while Jane rambled through the mountain meadows beside the lake, gathering wild flowers to arrange in garlands for their heads and in exotically fantastic bouquets.

Two days later Shelley counted his money and discovered that he had only twenty-eight pounds left. What was worse, he saw absolutely no prospect of obtaining more without returning to England to get it. "What to do?" Mary wrote in her journal. "It had cost us sixty to cross France from Paris to Neuchâtel."

After much discussion of their problem they acknowledged that they must return to England and must use a more economical manner of travel. Since water conveyances were cheapest, they determined to take advantage of the rivers to reach the coast. Shelley would have had them set out on their return journey the very next day, but because they had given their laundry to a village woman, they had to wait for it to be finished.

On the morning of the twenty-seventh they started back along the Lake of Lucerne. That evening, Jane, who had no wish to resume her humdrum life on Skinner Street, interrupted Shelley's reading aloud of Shakespeare by putting on one of her attacks of hysteria. Shelley was alarmed and distressed, but when he tried to reason her into calmness she screamed at him furiously. He had no *right* to manage his money so badly and spoil this journey for her! If she had known how many hardships she would have to suffer, they never could have persuaded her to come along in the first place.

Mary sat silent through it all. She knew very well that

it was of no use to reason with Jane in this mood, to remind her that she had *not* been persuaded by them to come but had practically forced her company upon them. This spell would pass, as Jane's "horrors" always did.

The next day they continued their travels by various small boats, water diligences, and public coaches until, on the evening of the twenty-ninth, they reached Basel on the river Rhine. From there they rode the great and storied stream, following its picturesque course between rocky hills and green vineyards. Below Mainz every eminence seemed to be crowned by a ruined castle. Mary's seventeenth birthday arrived while they were lodged in a dingy inn. "The day was not celebrated in comfort," Mary acknowledged in her journal. However, even if they "expected to be more at ease before her next anniversary," they could not possibly be any happier than they were at present, she added.

They left the river below Cologne, then traveled by diligence and post chaise over the sandy, level roads of Holland to Rotterdam. There they embarked at last and landed at Gravesend, England, on September 13. Shelley's purse was now completely empty. He could not even pay the boatman who had brought them up the river to London and had, therefore, to bring him along with them in the coach he hired to carry them to his bankers.

At the bank Shelley was given the dismaying news that Harriet had removed every penny from his account. Of course he had given her the right to draw from his funds, but he had not expected her to take it all! A tour of the city to borrow from various friends proved fruitless, while all the time the boatman and now, of course, the coachman grew more and more angry and abusive. Finally Shelley directed the driver to Harriet's house and, while Mary, Jane, the boatman, and the coachman waited outside, Shelley pleaded with his deserted wife for two long hours and finally emerged, triumphant, with twenty pounds.

He paid the men off, engaged rooms at a hotel, and then went out to buy some clothes for himself, for he was almost in rags. He also bought a copy of Wordsworth's *Excursion,* and they spent the evening reading and discussing the poet's lapse from the high, liberal principles of his youth. "He has become a slave!" Shelley declared.

The twenty pounds were soon gone. After that their troubles increased, for word of Shelley's return spread among his creditors. He was immediately besieged by bailiffs sent by the moneylenders from whom he had obtained the twelve hundred pounds for Godwin. Even when they moved from one lodging to another they were pursued and discovered, until, as winter approached, Shelley was forced to spend his nights with first one friend, then with another, for fear of being arrested and imprisoned for debt. In order to meet at all, he and Mary had to write notes to each other and plan secret trysts, sometimes in St. Paul's Cathedral, sometimes in Gray's Inn Gardens, sometimes, as before their elopement, beside her mother's grave.

Far from welcoming the prodigals home, the Godwins had refused to receive them at Skinner Street at all or to allow Fanny, newly returned from Dublin, to visit them. Moreover, the stories the Godwins had spread about their scandalous runaway had alienated many of Shelley's former friends. This did not, however, prevent Godwin from demanding the balance of the sum Shelley had promised, although he said he would not accept it from Shelley directly. All checks must be sent to him through a third person, for he scorned to have his name linked on paper with that of Shelley.

Nor would the philosopher believe that a young man who was heir to the vast Shelley fortune could not some-how raise the money he required. Godwin blandly acknowledged the fact that this could only be obtained in the form of a "post-obit," a loan to be paid back threefold when Shelley should come into his inheritance. It was this ruinous method, therefore, that Shelley began now to use, but even that took time.

Mrs. Godwin was willing to allow Jane to return home, but only on terms which the girl would not accept. Jane therefore remained with Mary and Shelley and added her peevishness and more and more frequent attacks of hysterical tantrums to what Mary was already enduring. Cut off from her family and friends and even from Shelley most of the time, Mary tried to fill her days with study. At Shelley's suggestion she had set herself to learn Greek, and now she worked at it doggedly, even when their landlady refused to furnish them with meals until their rent was paid. It was at this time that Jane suddenly decided to change her name to Claire, for "Claire Clairmont" had

such an exotic, romantic sound. She had lately been reading the poems of that blazing comet across the English
literary skies, Lord Byron, and she could talk only in terms
of romance.

In the midst of Mary's distress and confusion came the
news that on November 30 Harriet Shelley had given birth
to her expected child and that it was a son. Mary noted in
her journal Shelley's outspoken delight at this arrival. He
sent out circular letters to all who had ever been his friends
announcing the event. "Which ought to be ushered in
with the ringing of bells, etc. etc., for it is the son of his
wife," Mary wrote. If her words had a bitter tinge, it was
because Mary herself was now pregnant. She was suffering severely from morning nausea, moreover, which kept
her more than ever confined to their cramped, dingy
quarters.

Claire, as she now had to be called, soon grew bored
with staying indoors with the ailing Mary and chose instead to accompany Shelley on his many and various
errands around London. Mary struggled along with her
study of Greek in an all but hopeless effort to keep her
mind off her worries. Still desperately in love, she found
Shelley's absences harder than ever to bear when she knew
that the flighty Claire was with him. She told herself over
and over that jealousy was a base and disgraceful passion
in anyone who believed with Mary Wollstonecraft in the
complete freedom of love. But it tormented her none-
theless.

During November they had had a call from Shelley's

best friend of his Oxford days, Thomas Jefferson Hogg, who had shared Shelley's expulsion from the university because of their pamphlet *The Necessity of Atheism.* Since then Hogg had made his peace with his own father and was now settled in London as a barrister. He and Shelley had once quarreled over Hogg's too-marked attentions to Harriet, but now Shelley was willing to be friends with him again.

Mary rather disliked Hogg at first. For all his friendship for Shelley, no two men could have been less alike. He was engaging and well-read but also practical, commonplace, and earthy. He was devoted to Shelley and admired him extravagantly, but, like Shelley's other loyal friend, Peacock, he often jeered at Shelley's fantastic side, and this the blindly devoted Mary could not bear. He was warmhearted and kind, however, and Mary was now in great need of both these qualities, for she was not only ill from her pregnancy but also haunted by the terrifying knowledge that her mother had died in childbirth.

While Claire and Shelley were off on their countless jaunts around the city, Hogg took it upon himself to keep Mary's mind occupied by helping her with her Greek, discussing books with her, and listening sympathetically when she spoke of the harsh malevolence of Mamma, on whom all blame fell for her adored father's estrangement from her. At the house constantly, Hogg soon began the same sort of flirtation with Mary that he had had with Harriet—mild at first but increasingly ardent.

Shelley and Claire were undoubtedly having a love

affair, he told Mary. Since all four of them agreed on the absolute freedom of reasonable men and women to follow the dictates of their hearts, why should not he and Mary? Of course her pregnancy was an obstacle, now—but when that was over?

Mary was wholehearted in her loyalty to Shelley and refused to admit to Hogg that she had any cause to be jealous of Claire. She was the daughter of William God-win, however, and Hogg's arguments seemed logical to her and difficult to dispute. Mary's letters to him at this time show that, while she did not refuse his suggestions in so many words, she managed to put him off in a friendly and playful manner that would have done credit to an experienced coquette.

The year 1814 ended and 1815 began with Shelley still under the shadow of his debts. His constant moving about London left him no time for study or writing. This frustration made him so nervous and edgy that Mary, in her own ailing condition, found little comfort in their brief meetings. Still deeply in love, they flew into each other's arms at first sight; then, all too soon, out would come some irritable complaint or snappish rejoinder and bickering would start. These disputes were invariably stimulated by Claire, whose constant presence both Mary and Shelley now were finding more and more exasperating.

Then, early in January, came a change. Old Sir Bysshe Shelley died, Shelley's father became the baronet, and Shelley himself was now the heir to the title and fortune. It took almost six months of legal delays to settle the estate, however, and in the meantime the young man's situation seemed to grow even worse. His creditors now scented their money and were more importunate than ever. To escape their harassment, the trio moved their lodgings once again early in February, and there, on the twenty-second, Mary gave birth prematurely to a frail baby girl.

Mary stood the ordeal well, but the baby did not thrive. On March 2 they had to move again, and on the sixth the little creature died quietly in the night. True to her stoic training, Mary struggled to stifle her grief by reading and study, but nature was not to be denied. Her recovery was slow and her sleep was beset by dreams. In one of them it seemed to her that her child was not dead, only cold, and that by rubbing it before the fire they were able to bring it back to life. When she awoke to find it gone from her, she had to endure the agony of loss over again, and the next night the dream returned.

All that spring Claire's presence grew increasingly irksome. Her nagging and hysterics were wearing on Mary while she was beginning to recover her strength. Claire refused to go back to the Godwins even if they would have her, and she found excuses not to accept the few positions as a lady's companion that were offered to her. The one bright aspect of the situation was that Shelley and Mary were drawn closer together by their endeavors to solve what seemed a hopeless impasse. As for Hogg, with their reconciliation he quietly faded out of the picture.

Then, in May, Claire came mysteriously into some money—a prize in a lottery, she explained. She left them promptly and ensconced herself in a rose-covered cottage at Lynmouth. From there she wrote to Fanny, declaring how happy she was now in this peaceful new home away from the distressingly turbulent atmosphere that surrounded Mary and Shelley.

Mary commented in her diary on Claire's departure, writing that she was now starting a fresh volume of her journal "with our regeneration."

CHAPTER FIVE
1815 – 1816

The summer of 1815 began happily for Mary, for not only were she and Shelley free of the leechlike Claire but, in June, Sir Bysshe's estate was settled at last. Shelley was finally assured of a steady income of one thousand pounds a year together with a lump sum of seventy-five hundred pounds with which to pay his debts. This would have been ample for their needs if Shelley had not promptly signed over two hundred pounds a year to Harriet and if William Godwin had not continued his insatiable demands for funds.

With the fear now banished that Shelley might at any moment be arrested and dragged off to prison for debt, Mary's spirits soared, her health improved, and soon she was again the gay and radiant girl who had journeyed so lightheartedly through France and Switzerland the summer before.

The long strain had told on Shelley, however. He had lost so much weight and color that, at Mary's urging, he consulted a physician. When the doctor shook his head and spoke of a weakness in Shelley's chest, the dread word "consumption" sprang into Mary's mind and panic seized her. "We must leave London," she said. "We must find a healthier climate for you, a home in the country where you can take long walks through fields and woods. A quiet place where you can study and write."

They first went to the seaside in South Devon, then to Bristol. From there Shelley set off on house-hunting expeditions in search of a permanent home. In August he returned from one such quest in happy triumph, bringing news that he had found the ideal spot. "A furnished house at Bishopsgate near my friend Peacock's place at Marlow. It's on the edge of Windsor Great Park," he explained, his blue eyes sparkling. "Close to the ancient forest, so close that deer often come to graze before the door. The Thames flows nearby. I've engaged a skiff and I'll be able to boat to my heart's content."

Mary had found Peacock less than congenial, for his sluggish self-indulgence repelled her. She sensed, too, that he had been fond of Harriet and so disapproved of her own connection with Shelley. But during this past winter she had learned to appreciate his deep, undemonstrative kindliness. He might be gruff and cynical, incapable of enthusiasm, but he was also upright, conscientious, and shrewd. He too was a published writer of essays and novels, and Shelley was generous in his praise of Peacock's style. "His diction is characterized by lightness, strength, and chastity," Shelley said. Above all else from Mary's viewpoint, Peacock was helpful and loyal to Shelley.

At the end of their first month at Bishopsgate, Shelley,

Mary, Peacock, and Charles Clairmont, who had turned up for a visit, made a ten-day boat trip up the Thames. They started from Old Windsor and paused at Oxford, where Shelley showed Mary about his college haunts.

After their first full day of rowing Shelley had found himself so exhausted by the effort that he went to a local doctor for aid, but got no help from the medicine he prescribed. While they sat at supper in the low-raftered dining room of a village inn, Mary studied his drawn face in the candlelight and her heart sank. "Perhaps we should abandon our expedition," she said.

Peacock was eying Shelley's Spartan meal of tea, bread, and vegetables and his gaze was sardonic. "If you will allow me to prescribe for you I'll set you to rights," he asserted.

"What would be your prescription?" Shelley asked.

"Three mutton chops well peppered."

Shelley looked doubtful, for vegetarianism had become a part of his idealistic design for living. "Do you really think so?" he asked.

"I'm sure of it."

The waiter was summoned, the chops were broiled, and Shelley ate them without protest, even with some enjoyment. The result was all that Peacock had promised. Shelley's health improved almost overnight. He was able to row vigorously without tiring and "was cheerful, merry, overflowing with animal spirits," as Peacock recorded afterward.

Charles Clairmont too noted the change. "We have all felt the good effects of this jaunt," he wrote in a letter to his sister, Claire. "Shelley now has the ruddy, healthy complexion of autumn upon his countenance and he is twice as fat as he used to be."

During the long, bright days of early fall, Shelley set to work again upon a new, long poem. His theme was of a virtuous youth who was deluded by the evil Spirit of Solitude into sinking into self-centered seclusion and ultimate ruin. Its title, *Alastor,* was supplied by Peacock, who had a passion for all things Greek. Into it Shelley wove extraordinarily vivid descriptions of the scenery he had viewed in Switzerland or had glided past on the boating trip up the Thames.

When autumn brought its fruitful, golden days, Mary and Shelley relaxed into a quiet peace they had never before enjoyed. The house and its surroundings proved to be everything they had hoped for. Mary continued her Greek studies, Shelley his writing. He roamed the woods or floated dreamily on the river in his little skiff, a book always close at hand. Although they were still outcasts from Skinner Street and shunned by most of their former acquaintances, they had the company of a few loyal friends, notably Hogg, Peacock, and also Charles Clairmont. Grown to a pleasanter fellow than Mary would ever have expected, Charles often defied his mother's scoldings to visit them. Mary was now pregnant again, but she was suffering none of the discomfort that had plagued her before.

The neighborhood doctor whom she consulted proved to be a benevolent Quaker gentleman named Dr. Pope, of

Staines. He and Shelley held long philosophical discussions and even touched upon theology. Far from showing shock at Shelley's radical views, the good doctor listened to him gravely. "I like to hear thee talk, friend Shelley," he observed. "Thou art very deep."

When the evenings grew cold they sat before the fire and Shelley read aloud. He finished all the tragedies of Shakespeare and some of the comedies during those quiet months. His voice, which sometimes cracked and grew shrill in argument, was deep and pleasant when he read. Mary sewed contentedly on baby clothes beside him in the evenings and studied by day, giving very little thought to household affairs, for now they were able to hire a few servants. Although sadly incompetent by most standards, they managed to keep the Shelleys fed on the simple fare they required and to clean the house well enough to suit two young people whose thoughts were always on far higher matters.

As fall changed to winter some shadows began to gather in their bright world. Godwin renewed his demands for money and, at the same time, continued to denounce Shelley to his wide circle of followers. Claire, bored with her rural cottage and also low in funds, would have rejoined them if Shelley had not hastily sent her some money to keep her away. Claire then managed to coax her mother into receiving her at Skinner Street. While there in London she launched upon a harebrained scheme which was soon to have extraordinary consequences for Mary and Shelley as well as for herself.

Like many of the women in England at that time, Claire had long been dazzled from afar by the handsome and satanic poet Lord Byron. His heiress wife had now left him, and her hinted reasons for it were filling the papers with rumors of scandal and outright infamy. Claire had learned that Byron was one of the trustees of the famous Drury Lane Theatre, and she concocted a plan to obtain an interview with him. She wrote to him saying that she was an actress and begged his help in getting her a place in the Drury Lane Company.

After many failures, Claire at last succeeded in meeting Byron and attracting his roving eye. In triumph she boasted to Mary that she too had won the admiration of a poet—an infinitely more famous one than Shelley! He had actually written some verses in praise of her singing voice:

> There be none of Beauty's daughters
>   With a magic like thee;
> And like music on the waters
>   Is thy sweet voice to me . . .

To prove it all she took Mary with her on one of her visits to Byron. Mary too greatly admired Byron's work, but the meeting which Claire had arranged proved to be the briefest of passing glimpses. His lordship seemed to be in a bad humor at the time and paid them so little attention that Mary felt that the whole story might well have been one of Claire's fabricated romances.

During this pregnancy Shelley had tried to spare Mary's

feelings by withholding from her the knowledge of how spiteful the tone of her father's demanding letters to him had become. Mary, therefore, clung to her belief that it was solely due to Mamma's influence that her idolized father still treated her and Shelley like pariahs. When, on January 24, 1816, a healthy baby boy was born to her, she asked that the child be named for her father, and Shelley consented.

Thus the child was named William, a fact which Godwin noted with smugness in his journal. Immediately thereafter he dispatched another acid-worded claim upon Shelley's now badly overstrained purse. This time it was for funds to enable him to make a journey to Scotland, "partly for business, partly for a much-needed holiday," he wrote.

This was the last straw for Shelley, who had managed at last to pay off most of Godwin's debts. He rejoined with an indignant and reproachful and also typically exaggerated letter of refusal. "My blood boils in my veins, my gall rises against all that bear the human form when I think of what I, their benefactor and ardent lover, have endured of enmity and contempt from you and from all mankind!" Shelley wrote.

The young man's bitterness was aggravated by the coldness with which his newly published poem, *Alastor*, had been received. He had sent a copy, together with a personal letter, to his and Mary's former friend, the poet Southey. He had received no answer whatever, not even an acknowledgment, for Godwin had spread his venom only too well. A single review of *Alastor* appeared in the English press and even that was unfavorable. Shelley's work was still either ignored or reviled.

Shelley had expected to be criticized for his radical views by Tories and conservatives, but he had looked for different treatment from the liberal thinkers and writers who shared with him the philosophical beliefs of William Godwin and Mary Wollstonecraft. Their hostility was more than he could understand or endure. "We must either leave the country or find a home in the most distant and solitary regions of Cumberland or Scotland," he told Mary in black despair. "We get nothing but enmity and neglect here."

They were still in this mood of hurt bewilderment over his treatment by the English public when they had a visit from Claire. They received her reluctantly but were soon agreeably surprised to note a marked change in her. No longer flamboyant and opinionated, she was quiet, even docile, and she expressed the most affectionate sympathy for their troubles.

By a strange coincidence, Claire told them, she had heard very similar expressions of resentment against the bigotry of English society from Lord Byron, whose acquaintance she had made, as they knew. He was in fact soon leaving England behind him forever and planning to live in Geneva, Switzerland, where he hoped to find privacy and peace. Byron had told her that he had read Shelley's *Queen Mab* and had found it admirable, Claire added, almost as an afterthought.

"Byron admired *my* work!" Shelley's surprise and plea-

sure were so heartfelt and so humble that Mary felt a
surge of love and pity sweep through her. How all this
neglect and slander had hurt him! Someday, of course, the
world would recognize his genius—Mary had not the least
doubt of that. But in the meantime? She looked at Claire,
suddenly grateful beyond words for the brief happiness
the girl had brought to her beloved by repeating Byron's
praise.

Then an idea came to her, so shining-clear that it was on
her lips in an instant. They too must go to Europe. They
must leave this country and their tormentors far behind.
And why not to Geneva, where Shelley could meet Lord
Byron and share thoughts and philosophies with him?

The three discussed the question at length with more
and more enthusiasm. By April 25, when the papers were
full of Lord Byron's dramatic and final departure from
England, their minds were settled. It took Shelley little
more than a week after that to make his arrangements. On
May 3 they sailed from Dover with baby William and also
Claire, for she had easily convinced Shelley that her acquaintance with Lord Byron would ensure him a meeting
with the famous exile.

To please Mary, Shelley composed a letter of farewell
to her father before they left. He explained his motives in
departing from his native land, perhaps forever. In closing
he expressed his continuing admiration for Godwin's
teachings and even went so far as to ask his forgiveness
for the bitter tone of his recent letters.

They reached Paris on May 8 and proceeded by the same route they had followed earlier to Troyes. Then through Auxerre, Dijon, Dôle, and over the Jura Mountains. As they entered Geneva at last in the gathering dusk, snow was falling against the windows of their coach, shutting off their view of the lake and the Alps beyond it. Soon the storm cleared, and by May 17 they looked out upon a bright summer scene from their hotel at Sécheron.

They engaged a Swiss girl named Elise to care for little William, and Shelley at once hired a boat for excursions upon the clear blue waters that lapped the shore. "Every evening about six o'clock we sail upon the lake, which is delightful," Mary wrote to a friend. "The waves of this lake never afflict me with that sickness that deprives me of all enjoyment of a sea voyage; on the contrary, the tossing of the boat but raises my spirits and inspires me with unusual hilarity.

"We do not enter society here, yet our time passes swiftly and delightfully. We read Latin and Italian during the heats of noon and when the sun declines we walk in the gardens of the hotel. . . . I feel as happy as a new-fledged bird and care not what twig I fly to, so that I may try my new-found wings."

William was rosy and healthy, Shelley seemed to have forgotten all his cares, and Claire not only was the pleasantest of companions but was also proving a helpful one by copying Shelley's letters for him. No wonder Mary felt that she was living in a delightful dream.

Then, on May 25, they returned from an excursion to find a huge, ornate coach drawn up before the door of their hotel. Three menservants were unloading it and a crowd had gathered, mostly made up of British tourists. Word was passing among them that the coach belonged to the famous and notorious nobleman Lord Byron!

CHAPTER SIX
1816

The proprietor of the hotel had come out to supervise the unloading of the baggage, and the throng of onlookers immediately inundated him with questions. Yes, the two gentlemen who had disappeared so swiftly inside the hotel were indeed Lord Byron and his physician, Dr. Polidori, he told them. "His lordship has given me orders that he's not to be disturbed. He has refused to receive calls or messages either. Especially none from any of his fellow countrymen," he added with an apologetic shrug.

This last news dismayed and disappointed Shelley, who had already written a letter to be handed to Lord Byron upon his arrival, inviting him to dinner. He received no reply to that, but, a few evenings later, when Mary and Shelley were enjoying the air in the hotel garden, Byron appeared and came toward them accompanied by his doctor. Byron was dressed casually in a green jacket and light-colored cotton trousers. He carried a cane and walked with a slight limp, and he was smiling as he held out his hand to Shelley. Mary recognized him at once—there was no mistaking the splendid, classic contours of that face and head she had seen so briefly before. But how much more dazzling now, cordial and animated, Mary thought as the two men greeted each other.

"Mad, bad and dangerous to know," one of his titled mistresses in England had said of Lord Byron, but no one could be more engaging than he when he chose. He seemed already to have formed a high opinion of Shelley's work, and it was soon clear that Shelley the man pleased him no less. It was clear, too, as he bowed over Mary's hand like a courtier, that he did not remember his previous meeting with her. At the bold look of admiration in his luminous gray eyes her heartbeat quickened and her cheeks grew warm in spite of her determination not to let herself be enmeshed by his famous charm. Claire appeared a few minutes later. Byron greeted her with a polite but slightly distant acknowledgment of their acquaintance. Claire curtseyed demurely, lowering her lashes before young Dr. Polidori's inquiring glance, and sat down beside Mary.

And so began a magical summer which Mary was to recall the rest of her life, often with joy, sometimes with tears. The conversation started that evening between the two rebel-poets was the first of many, and the sound of those two voices—Shelley's eager, rapid, and high-pitched, Byron's deeper and more deliberate—fixed itself in her mind forever.

For all his pose of aristocratic indifference, Byron worked vigorously at his writing. He was busy every morning with new cantos of his already world-famous *Childe*

Harold's Pilgrimage, but in the afternoons and evenings he sought Shelley's companionship. Contact with Byron's thinking, so different from his own yet so like in originality and power, roused and stimulated Shelley. His spirits rose as if on wings, his long period of frustration ended: soon he was writing again. The evenings of talk ranged widely over literature, philosophy, and politics, and they often lasted until dawn. Too shy and unsure of herself to enter into the discussions, Mary sat, starry-eyed, drinking in every word and storing it all away in her memory.

Byron shared Shelley's love of boating. He was immediately invited to join their expeditions on the lake, either scudding before the wind or drifting idly on the still evening waters that mirrored the stars so clearly in their dark depths. Byron was full of fascinating stories of his travels in Greece, Turkey, and Albania.

"Shall I sing you an Albanian song?" he asked on one such starlit evening. "Now be sentimental and give me all of your attention." What he gave forth was a strange, wild howl, so loud and terrifying that both Mary and Claire gasped in fright. Byron laughed at their surprise. "It's an exact imitation of the savage Albanian mode," he assured them. "I suppose you expected some plaintive, minor, Eastern love melody?" It was from Byron's fondness for all things Albanian that Mary and Claire soon gave him the nickname Albe. Only among themselves, however, for they soon learned that for all his liberal views Byron set great store by rank and must always be addressed by his title.

Shelley soon became irked by the stares and whispers of

the tourists who thronged the hotel to have a look at the wicked English lord and his young friends. At the end of May he moved his party across the narrow end of the lake to a small cottage, the Maison Chapuis, near Coligny. Every evening after that Byron and Polidori rowed the short distance to join the Shelleys for dinner. On one such occasion, as he was starting off under a cloudy night sky to return to Sécheron, Byron began to sing the Tyrolese Song of Liberty written by his friend Tom Moore. The sound was carried back for a long time over the water by the rising wind until finally it faded away softly into the dark distance. Mary was to describe those moments of romantic, unforgettable beauty many years later to Tom Moore himself.

Two weeks after the Shelleys' move, Byron followed their example and rented a large, handsome country house, the Villa Deodati, on the hillside just above them. Only a terraced vineyard lay between their houses. By this time Dr. Polidori had revealed himself as a conceited, long-winded young bore who insisted on injecting his shallow comments into all conversations. He was also touchy, easily offended, and wildly jealous of Lord Byron's new interest in Shelley. Byron tolerated his foibles good-naturedly, nicknamed him Polly-dolly, and remarked with a smile that "a great part of my time is spent in looking after my own medical attendant."

When Shelley and Polidori engaged in a sailing race and Shelley won it, the doctor accused him of unfair tactics and challenged him to a duel. Shelley merely laughed and ignored the challenge, but Byron turned upon the small, furious fellow. "Recollect that though Shelley has some scruples against dueling, I have none," he said. "I shall be at all times ready to take his place." Polidori sulked but he made no answer. He knew only too well that Byron was entirely ruthless and was also an excellent shot.

Soon after this the fine weather ended and rain kept the party indoors for many days. One stormy evening when the wind shook the shutters and the candle flames flared on the table, the talk turned to ghosts and ghost stories. Polidori had found a volume of eerie tales in the villa's library, and the group read them aloud by turns, discussing each at length. "Any one of us could do better than those, even our quiet little Mary here," Byron exclaimed at last. "Yes, and to prove it we must each write a ghost story. All four of us, remember. You and I shall publish ours together, Mary," he added. It amused him to see Mary's shy, startled look when he addressed her directly.

The next evening each of the three men reported his progress. Byron's was a tale about a vampire, which he used afterward as part of a long poem. Shelley's was based on a frightening childhood experience, but he soon abandoned it. Polidori embarked upon a full-length novel concerned with a skull-headed lady who peeped through keyholes at her victims. Only Mary could think of no subject horrifying enough to use, and each day she had to admit, in answer to Byron's jovial, probing queries, that she had nothing to report.

Then one night the conversation centered on questions

about the primal source of life itself and whether there was any probability that it would ever be discovered and communicated. Shelley, always interested in scientific speculations, spoke of some recent experiments he had read about. "Perhaps a corpse could somehow be reanimated; galvanism has given a hint of such a possibility," he said. "Perhaps the component parts of a creature might be manufactured, brought together, and endued with vital warmth." The talk went on in this vein until long past midnight.

Mary could not fall asleep that night. She closed her eyes, but her imagination had been stirred and now a series of pictures went racing through her mind, pictures far too vivid to erase. She recorded the entire experience later in detail. "I saw—with shut eyes but with acute mental vision —I saw the pale student of unhallowed arts kneeling beside the thing he had put together—I saw the hideous phantasm of a man stretched out, and then, on the working of some powerful engine, show signs of life, and stir with an uneasy, half-vital, motion. Frightful it must be. . . . his success would terrify the artist; he would rush away from his odious handiwork, horror-stricken. He would hope that, left to itself, the slight spark he had communicated would fade; that this thing, which had received such imperfect animation, would subside into dead matter; and he might sleep in the belief that the silence of the grave would quench forever the transient existence of this hideous corpse which he had looked upon as the cradle of life. He sleeps; but he is wakened; he opens his eyes; behold, the horrid thing stands at his bedside, opening the curtains and looking on him with yellow, watery, speculative eyes.

"I opened mine in terror. The idea so possessed my mind that a thrill of fear ran through me, and I wished to exchange the ghastly image of my fancy for the realities around. I see them still; the very room, the dark parquet, the closed shutters, with the moonlight struggling through, and the sense I had that the glassy lake and the white high Alps were beyond. I could not so easily get rid of my hideous phantom; still it haunted me. I must try to think of something else. I recurred to my ghost story—my tiresome unlucky ghost story. Oh! If I could only contrive one which would frighten my readers as I myself had been frightened that night!

"Swift as lightning and as cheering was the idea that broke in upon me. 'I have found it! What terrified me will terrify others; and I need only describe the spectre which haunted my midnight pillow.' On the morrow I announced that *I had thought of a story*. I began that day with the words *It was a dreary night in November*, making only a transcript of the grim terrors of my waking dream."

Mary had thought at first of fashioning merely a short story, but when she told it to Shelley the idea so intrigued him that he persuaded her to develop it into a full-length book. And so it was that Mary, at eighteen, began to write her still-famous novel, *Frankenstein, or the Modern Prometheus*.

In mid-June, Shelley and Byron decided to make a cruise around the shores of Lake Leman, together with two boatmen and a servant. Dr. Polidori had expected to go with them, but, most conveniently for the others, he injured his foot the day before they were to start and was forced to stay behind. Mary had expressed some misgivings about the trip, reminding them all that Shelley had never learned to swim. "You need have no fear for him, Mary," Lord Byron assured her. "I can swim well enough for both of us."

Byron was as inordinately proud of his prowess at swimming as he was of his marksmanship, and he never tired of describing his famous swim across the Hellespont. But now Shelley smiled and shook his head. "I'd far rather drown outright than have you endanger your life to save mine," he said.

On their tour the two poets visited the many storied towns that bordered the lake—Clarens, alive with memories of Rousseau, whose philosophy Shelley admired; Lausanne, where Gibbon had written his mighty *History of the Decline and Fall of the Roman Empire;* and the Ferney of Voltaire. The grim water-side Castle of Chillon made a profound impression upon them both. The evening after they visited it, Byron wrote the whole of his *Prisoner of Chillon,* while Shelley began to compose his noble *Hymn to Intellectual Beauty.*

During this cruise Shelley introduced Byron to Wordsworth's early writing. Until that time Byron had refused to read any of that poet's work, but Shelley's enthusiasm was infectious. Although he scoffed afterward at Shelley's "dosing me with Wordsworth," Byron was impressed in spite of himself and for a time thereafter Wordsworth's influence noticeably colored his own poetry.

While they were away, Mary worked hard on the first draft of *Frankenstein* and Claire continued with her copying of Shelley's voluminous letters, most of them addressed to Peacock. Claire was still the quiet, agreeable girl she had been since they left England, Mary noted with satisfaction. Her penmanship was excellent, and now even Lord Byron was willing to let her cross the vineyard to the Villa Deodati almost every day to transcribe what he had completed of *Childe Harold*'s Third Canto.

The voyagers returned by the first of July. Shelley was filled to overflowing with the splendors of the mountain scenery he had viewed. Weeks of quiet reading, talking, and writing came after this, with more evenings on the water until another siege of rain kept them indoors. When the weather cleared again, Shelley took Mary and Claire on a short trip to Chamonix at the foot of Mont Blanc to see the great glaciers, notably the Mer de Glace, and also to the source of the river Arveyron. Mary brought her *Frankenstein* manuscript along with her and worked on it in the evenings after long days of travel by muleback, with the result that the Vale of Chamonix forms a dramatic background for part of her novel.

By July 28, "the second anniversary of our union," as Mary recorded happily in her journal, they were back in the Maison Chapuis and had resumed their routine of study, translation, and writing. Shelley's birthday came on August 6. Mary had bought him a telescope for a present and, remembering his boyish delight in fireworks, she toiled over the making of a fire balloon to be sent up over the lake. That evening, in the gayest of spirits, the whole party rowed out to launch it, only to find that there was too much wind. They returned to land and sent the balloon up from the shore, but it caught fire almost as soon as it left the ground.

The disappointment in Shelley's uplifted face as he watched the charred fragments fall gave Mary a surprisingly sharp pang of regret and sympathy. It was as though this small disaster symbolized for him some larger failure, a failure of hopes that once had promised to soar brightly upward to unimagined heights.

Letters had been arriving from Fanny all summer, long letters full of news of the Godwin circle. Coleridge was now living with an apothecary who was doing his best to keep the poet from overindulging in either drugs or drink, but with little success, Fanny wrote. As for Coleridge's newly published poem, *Kubla Khan,* "Mr. Lamb says that it was written in his sleep and is nonsense." Fanny herself had been reading all of Lord Byron's published poetry, and she asked innumerable questions about the man himself. Did he actually visit them in their own house and invite them to his? What was he *really* like?

Fanny described, too, the misery that unemployment had brought to English workers this year, and Mr. Robert Owen's plans for relieving it. He had made a speech before the newly formed "Institution for the Formation of Character" in which he advocated measures to ensure that "no human being shall work more than two or three hours every day; that all shall be equal; that no one shall dress but after the plainest and simplest manner; that they be allowed to follow any religion, as they please; and that their studies shall be Mechanics and Chemistry." Although Fanny felt sick at heart over the sufferings of the poor, she could not believe that such a society as Owen promoted "could possibly produce poets, painters or philosophers."

Mr. Owen was nevertheless a great and good man, Fanny declared. "He told me the other day that he wished our Mother were living, as he had never before met with a person who thought so exactly as he did, or who would have so warmly and zealously entered into his plans." Did Mary agree with this description of their mother's teachings? Fanny was inclined to think that Mr. Owen was perhaps mistaken in this.

This letter, like all of Fanny's, contained a plaintive and detailed account of Godwin's monetary affairs and an anxious plea for assistance from Shelley. How could Mary recount so gaily the pleasant details of their life there on the shores of the idyllic Lake Leman? Fanny asked her reproachfully. "You know the peculiar temperature of Papa's mind. You know he cannot write when pecuniary circumstances overwhelm him; you know that it is of the utmost consequence, for his *own* and the *world's sake* that he should finish his novel; and is it not your and Shelley's duty to consider these things and to endeavor to prevent, as far as lies in your power, giving him unnecessary pain and anxiety?"

Shelley shook his head helplessly over this message. Their own money had been running low and bad news had come recently from his London solicitor. If Shelley expected to receive the half-yearly payment of his income from his grandfather's estate, he must appear in England to accept it in person. "Back to England?" Mary cried in dismay. "Can't it be arranged in some other way?"

"I'm afraid it's impossible," he answered. He was looking out at the bright shimmer of water, and the shadow of parting from all that beauty and peace was already darkening his blue eyes.

He's been so happy here, and so well, Mary thought, remembering the doctor's grave face when he had spoken of "a weakness of the lungs." It's wrong, it's wicked to expose him to that English climate again. "Perhaps you could make the trip a short one and return quickly," she suggested.

They discussed this idea for some days, meanwhile continuing their routine. M. G. Lewis, the noted author of *The Monk* and other eerie Gothic novels, had recently arrived at Byron's villa. Lewis had only just returned from a visit to estates he had inherited in Jamaica, and he was filled with horror at the wickedness of the slave trade. While in Jamaica he had done his best to improve the condition of his own blacks, and now he asked Byron, Shelley, and Polidori to sign their names as witnesses to an addition he was making to his will. In it he forbade his heir to sell any of his slaves and stipulated that the new owner must visit the estate in person for three months out of every year.

Shelley praised Lewis warmly for this, but he still argued with him over his cynical view of the spectral mysteries which formed the subjects of his books. Both Lewis and Byron scoffed at Shelley's feeling that such things might well exist. They maintained that a belief in ghosts implied belief in God and immortality. Shelley, as an avowed atheist, could not logically hold to such opinions, they told him.

For his part, Shelley considered this unreasonable. What was more, he contended that most people who professed scornful disbelief in ghosts by daylight thought far more respectfully of the world of shadows when night approached.

These sessions of talk with Lewis diverted Shelley for a time from the problem of his return to England. Besides, any mention of leaving Switzerland sent Claire immediately into moodiness and gloom. Then one evening, quite without warning, she went into one of her old fits of hysterics and sobbed out the shattering news that she was pregnant, pregnant by Lord Byron. Their affair had begun in April, in London. Claire had long been in love with Byron's image from afar, and her application to him for a part in a Drury Lane play had been only an excuse to meet him and to fling herself into his arms.

When she learned that he was leaving England almost immediately, she had begged to go with him, but, after that one brief liaison, he had refused brutally to have anything more to do with her. When she wrote to him again, vowing that she would follow him to Switzerland, he had replied that he would decline to see her if she came there alone and unprotected. She had then persuaded Shelley and Mary to travel to Geneva solely to bring her with them. She had determined to confront Byron once again and to compel him to make a monetary settlement on her and her expected child. This, in spite of all her pleas, he still refused to do.

Appalled to silence, Mary and Shelley looked at each other, both shaken to the core. Yet what could they say? Did not they both uphold and, what was more, practice before the world complete liberty to love? Yes, to *love*. But was not this utterly different from their free and happy union—this selfish, wild passion so quickly turned to quarreling and now to a sordid demand for money? *Surely, surely this was different,* Mary's heart insisted desperately, but a small, clear voice somewhere within her refused to be entirely deceived, and in Shelley's face she could see the reflection of her own emotions.

And here was Claire, sobbing before them. Whether or not she had brought this upon herself by her own folly, she was here, a girl of eighteen under their protection, helpless, penniless, and, except for them, alone in a world that could be unspeakably cruel. What use were reproaches and recriminations now? The fact of her plight faced them. They must shelter her as best they could.

Mary drew a deep, shaking breath as though she were

shouldering a new and heavy burden, took Claire in her arms, and looked across the disheveled dark head up into Shelley's face. The flush of anger was gone and now it was full of sorrow and pity. How good, how gentle, how generous he is, she thought, her heart overflowing with love and gratitude that she was allied to such a man.

"I will have to talk with Lord Byron," Shelley said. "It will be a difficult interview, but I will do what I can."

CHAPTER SEVEN
1816

Shelley took the steep path they had all climbed so often up through the vineyard to the Villa Deodati, but this time there was no spring or buoyancy to his step. When he returned late in the evening, he reported to Mary that Lord Byron had remained friendly and courteous throughout the interview and had freely admitted Claire's charges. Byron had declared, however, that her pursuit of him, her following him here to Switzerland, her demands, and her ill-tempered tantrums of late had driven away any sympathy or affection he had ever had for her. "I was never in love with her," Byron stated baldly. Now he wanted no more to do with her. He had begun to dislike her heartily, and his aversion grew each time he saw her.

Byron's harsh cynicism shocked and repelled the gentle-hearted Shelley, but what could he say? He himself had heard Claire's wild confession from her own lips, and he was far too honest to reproach Byron or to plead Claire's cause even if he thought it would do any good. Finally, however, when Shelley brought up the question of providing for his child, he saw Byron's face soften. Byron would still promise nothing definite, but Shelley let the matter rest there and did not press for a firm commitment. Remembering Byron's often stated love for his small daughter, Ada, whom he was never allowed to see since his separation from his wife, Shelley returned down through the moonlit vineyard bringing some small measure of hope on that score from the painful confrontation.

It was now certain that they must all return to England, and soon. They were in even greater need of money than ever, since it appeared that Claire must be a fixture in their household once again. Where else could she go? Not to Skinner Street, certainly—they were all desperately determined to hide any knowledge of her condition from the Godwins as long as possible. They therefore decided to settle as far from London as was practicable. Why not stay in the city of Bath, where they were all unknown, until the birth of Claire's child?

Mary's journal records that the last week of August was spent in packing and, on August 29, the day before Mary's nineteenth birthday, they set forth toward the seaport of Le Havre. There were five in their party—Shelley, Mary, Claire, baby William, and the Swiss nursemaid, Elise. With him Shelley was bringing three manuscripts which Lord Byron had entrusted to his care—the Third Canto of *Childe Harold, The Prisoner of Chillon,* and *Manfred.*

On their way to Le Havre they stopped at Versailles, whose opulent splendors Shelley compared unfavorably with the classic simplicity of Athens. Their chief interest in the palace was to see where one of the dramas of the French Revolution had taken place—the capture of Louis XVI and his queen by the Paris mob. They paused again in Rouen to visit the cathedral which housed the tomb of Richard the Lion-Hearted, crusader-king of England, and one of Shelley's boyhood heroes.

The start of their crossing of the Channel was delayed for several days by storms. When they finally sailed, their vessel was so beaten about by contrary winds that it took twenty-six hours to reach Portsmouth. Mary suffered as wretchedly as ever from seasickness. She had barely recovered when she had to take the responsibility for getting the family by coach to Bath while Shelley hurried up to London to transact his business. Once in their rooms at 5 Abbey Church Road, Bath, Mary collapsed, worn out by the journey. Baby William was fretful, Elise was so homesick that she joined in his tears, while Claire railed bitterly against life in general and Lord Byron in particular. Soon Mary's exhaustion took a form which it was to assume so often after that, of deep depression and a dark and looming presentiment of disaster.

When the others were settled in reasonable comfort, Mary joined Shelley, who was staying with Peacock at Marlow. She went hopefully and remained there for two weeks, but the place soon lost its charm for her because Shelley, to whom in her weakened state she clung desperately for reassurance, had to spend most of his time in London. He was occupied there not only with his own affairs but also in negotiating as Byron's agent with his publisher, John Murray, for the three manuscripts he had brought with him from Switzerland. He succeeded in the matter so well that he was able to report to Byron that he would receive two thousand guineas for the poems—an astronomical sum to poor Shelley. "I seem to be able to bargain very shrewdly in someone else's behalf," he told Mary with a rueful smile. "But then, Byron has astonishing powers. If only they could be exerted to their full extent for good!"

By this time Godwin had learned of their return and was renewing his demands for money. Late in September, Fanny met Shelley by arrangement in Piccadilly with a plea for her father couched in such pitiful terms that Shelley somehow managed to scrape up another two hundred pounds for him. "Fanny seemed so unhappy and distraught that I could not refuse her," Shelley reported to Mary. "But of course we are both familiar with her worrying nature."

Back in Bath again, Mary took up her work on *Franken-stein* as well as her study of Greek and Latin. She also embarked on something new—drawing lessons from a local artist, a Mr. West. Baby William, or "the Willmouse" —Mary's pet name for him—was now healthy and lively once more and Elise cheerful again. Claire's moods were as unpredictable as ever, but Shelley had procured a piano for her which gave her far more pleasure than it did those who had to listen to her loud and constant playing.

Things seemed at last to be running with relative smoothness when, early in October, a long, melancholy letter came from Fanny. Papa had needed three hundred pounds instead of the two hundred Shelley had sent him, and he was therefore unable to write a word on his novel. Mamma's grumbling never ceased, nor could Fanny blame her, for she, Fanny, was of no use at all to them or to anyone else. In fact, she was nothing but a burden on those whom she loved.

Greatly distressed, Mary started as loving and comforting an answer as she could frame, but before it could be sent another letter arrived from Fanny. It was dated October 9 and it came from Bristol. Fanny had left London forever, she stated. She was entirely alone in the world now that she had neither Claire nor Mary for sisters, nor Shelley for a friend—he who had once and so briefly brightened her life. Mamma's tirades against Mary and Shelley and all they stood for had become more than Fanny could bear. Worst of all, Mamma had just informed her that Godwin, whom she had loved and revered all her life, was not her father at all! In complete astonishment, Mary read on.

Fanny was the child of her mother's previous union, the letter continued. One Gilbert Imlay, an American, was her father, but he had long ago deserted his family and returned to his native land. Crushed under this final blow, Fanny had decided to "depart immediately to the dark spot from which I hope never to remove."

Shocked and alarmed, Shelley rushed off to Bristol while Mary waited in an agony of apprehension. He was haggard and weary when he returned at two o'clock in the morning with no news of the missing girl. After the briefest rest he started off again. Two days of searching revealed tragedy. On October 9 Fanny had taken lodgings at the Hackworth Arms, in Swansea, and the next morning the chambermaid had found her lying lifeless on her bed with an empty laudanum bottle beside her.

Fanny had left a letter, her last one. In it she bid a pathetic farewell to the world and expressed the hope that those to whom the news of her death might perhaps give some pain would soon be eased of it by forgetting that she had ever existed. The note was unsigned, and a watch which Mary had sent to her from Geneva was lying on top of it.

William Godwin had also received a letter sent by Fanny from Bristol, and he too had traced her and learned the dreadful truth. Godwin had always expressed exactly the same feeling for Fanny as for the other children, and in the midst of her grief Mary's heart ached for him too. She wrote him a loving and sympathetic letter and received an immediate reply. It was her first communication from him since her elopement, and Mary opened it gratefully, forgetting and forgiving his harsh rejection of her during these past years. Surely that had all been Mamma's fault, she told herself once again.

Sympathy would be of no service to him, Godwin wrote, but he accepted it nevertheless. What would be of real help would be for her to aid him in avoiding all publicity over this sad affair. "Do not go to Swansea, disturb not the silent dead; do nothing to destroy the obscurity she so much desired," he bade Mary. His chief fear was of what might be said about it in the papers. He had decided to explain to everyone that Fanny had started for Ireland to visit her aunts—a trip she had talked of for some time. On the way there she had stopped in Wales with friends, had there developed an inflammatory fever, and had died of it. This story would ensure that there could be no unfavorable reflection upon the Godwin family.

The fact that her adored father had written to her at last was of some help, but her anguish over Fanny's death lingered with Mary. She was tormented by the thought that if she herself had not been so wrapped up in her own affairs she might have sensed Fanny's despair and somehow helped her to overcome it. Shelley felt the same bitter regrets. He reproached himself with special sharpness because he had seen Fanny only a few weeks before, had noted her sadness, yet had done nothing about it. The memory of Fanny's pale, pinched little face as she bade him goodbye in London so preyed upon him that it made him actually ill, for to feel himself morally at fault in any way was a shattering experience for the sensitive Shelley. Claire, who had seldom given a moment's thought to Fanny or her troubles, now proclaimed herself prostrate with grief and took to her bed. It remained for Mary, then, to summon all her fortitude, to try to contain her own sorrow, and to supply what comfort and steadiness she could to her emotion-wracked family.

It became necessary to change their lodgings to rooms in New Bond Street, and while Mary managed the move she sent Shelley off to Peacock in Marlow, partly for a rest and partly in the hope that he would find them a permanent residence. In a note written at this time she begged him "not to be too quick or attach yourself too much to one spot . . . a house with a lawn, near a river or lake, noble trees or divine mountains, a garden and *absentia* Claire" would be her ideal choice.

While the weeks dragged on and the birth of Claire's child drew near, Mary did her best to dispel her continuing depression by writing and study. Then, early in December, some good news arrived for a change. Shelley learned that Leigh Hunt of *The Examiner* had published an article giving favorable notice to three young poets, Keats, Shelley, and Reynolds. In it Hunt wrote of all three that he "rejoiced that some few poets of the day were wise enough to go directly to Nature for Inspiration." About Shelley in particular he wrote, "Of the first who came before us we have, it is true, seen only one or two specimens. . . . we shall procure what he has published and if the rest answer to what we have seen, we shall have no hesitation in announcing him for a very striking and original thinker. His name is Percy Bysshe Shelley and he is the author of a poetical work, *Alastor, or the Spirit of Solitude.*"

The effect of this praise upon Shelley was electric. He called upon Hunt at once, had a long talk with him, and thus began a cordial and enduring friendship. Shelley was radiant when he returned to Bath on December 14. He described his meeting with Hunt at Hampstead in enthusiastic detail. "I have not in all my intercourse with mankind experienced sympathy and kindness with which I have been so affected or which my whole being has so sprung forward to meet," he told Mary.

At Hunt's home Shelley was introduced to his fellow recipient of Hunt's praises, young John Keats. The two poets had enjoyed a long walk together over Hampstead Heath. Shelley had told Keats of his admiration for his work and had also offered him some well-meant criticism and advice—both of which Keats had received with courteous but cool reserve. Hunt later expressed the opinion that Keats was overly conscious of the fact that Shelley was the son of a baronet, resented the difference in their social stations, and felt that he was being patronized.

Hunt had praised Peacock's writings also, and Shelley informed him of his and Peacock's long friendship. He hoped to introduce those two to each other soon in his new home, Shelley told Mary. At last they had found and leased a comfortable dwelling, Albion House at Great Marlow, near wooded hills, sweet green fields, and a delightful river. Best of all, it was spacious enough to permit ample room for their friends to visit. It was to be ready for them early in February.

The next morning's post brought a letter to Shelley from Hookham, his business agent. Shelley opened it eagerly. He had commissioned Hookham to get in touch with Harriet and try to persuade her to let their children, Ianthe and Charles, visit Shelley in his new home.

Watching him eagerly as he read the letter, Mary saw

his face turn suddenly ashen. He handed the sheet of paper to her without a word, and as she read it, she felt herself grow weak. On the previous Tuesday, Harriet's body had been found in the Serpentine, the stream which flows through Hyde Park in London. "She was called 'Harriet Smith,'" Hookham wrote, "and the verdict was 'Found drowned.'"

Mary was too stunned to speak, but Shelley was already on his feet. "The children!" he exclaimed. "I must claim them before her detestable family, the Westbrooks, can get their hands on them." And he was off to London.

The next day's post brought Mary the first of several long, frantic, and impassioned letters in which Shelley gave her the details of Harriet's pitiful story. She had been driven from her father's house "by the cruelty of her family," Shelley wrote. She had taken rooms in the house of a Mrs. Jane Thomas in the Chelsea section of London, giving her name as Harriet Smith. On November 9 she had disappeared from there and had not been seen alive since. These were the bare facts. It seemed certain that she had taken her own life, and the reasons for that were grim and dark indeed, Shelley hinted to Mary.

He had not yet got custody of his children. They had not been with Harriet in London but, for some time past, had been in Warwick in the care of a clergyman-school-teacher, the Reverend Mr. Kendall.

Leigh Hunt was with him constantly, Shelley wrote, and was helping him through the strain of this terrible ordeal. Shelley had visited a lawyer, a Mr. Longdil, about securing the guardianship of his children, and Longdil had advised him that it would be wise for him and Mary to go through a legal marriage at once, so that if it became necessary to take the case of child custody to court, their unsanctioned living together could not be used against him. "A mere nominal union, after your having blessed me with a life, a world of real happiness!" Shelley commented.

Mary answered his letter promptly. "These Westbrooks! But they have nothing to do with your sweet babes; they are yours and I do not see the pretense of any suit." As to the marriage: "Be governed by your friends as to when it ought to take place, but it must be in London, not Bath. Come back soon and bring your darling Ianthe and Charles. Thank your kind friends, and I long to hear news about Godwin."

At Mary's request but with some apprehension Shelley made a call upon the Godwin household. Mary's father received him very coldly at first, but when he learned that Shelley planned actually to wed his daughter, the philosopher who had written so scathingly against the institution of marriage faced about abruptly. He himself hurried to arrange the time and place for the wedding at the earliest possible date, December 30, at St. Mildred's in Bread Street. Mrs. Godwin lost no time either. She invited the young couple to stay at Skinner Street with them when they came up to town for the ceremony.

Shortly afterward Godwin wrote to his brother, who lived in Hull and whom he had ignored for years. "My daughter is between nineteen and twenty. The piece of news I have to tell, however, is that I went to church with this tall girl some little time ago to be married. Her husband is the eldest son of Sir Timothy Shelley of Field Place in the county of Sussex, Baronet. So that, according to the vulgar ideas of the world, she is well married and I have great hopes the young man will make her a good husband. You will wonder, I dare say, how a girl without a penny of fortune should meet with so good a match. But such are the ups and downs of this world."

Shelley himself sent news of the ceremony to Claire, commenting that "Godwin throughout has shown the most polished and courteous attention to me and to Mary. He seems to think no kindness too great in compensation for what has passed. I confess that I am not entirely deceived by this."

But Mary, now back at last in her beloved father's good graces, glowed with happiness. As always, she was almost completely blind to imperfections in those she cared for, and she was full of plans for receiving Ianthe and Charles into her family, the sooner the better.

CHAPTER EIGHT
1816 – 1818

To Shelley's amazed indignation, Harriet's family, the Westbrooks, refused to give up Ianthe and Charles to him. Instead they filed a lawsuit in which they asked that the children be made Wards in Chancery and that the court then appoint a suitable person to act as their guardian. The arguments they gave were a bitter indictment of Shelley. They declared that he was an unfit person to have the charge or the education of his children, and they cited their reasons. He was a follower of the infamously radical philosopher William Godwin. He had deserted his lawful wife, Harriet, and this cruelty had led to her untimely death. He had been living shamelessly in unsanctioned union with one Mary Godwin. He was an avowed atheist, as shown by his writings. The Lord Chancellor did not reject the Westbrooks' suit outright, as Shelley had optimistically expected, but set a date, January 24, for hearing the case.

It was with this heavy threat hanging over them that Mary and Shelley returned to Bath. There, on January

12, 1817, Claire gave birth to a baby girl, whom she named Alba, and for the moment there was rejoicing over her safe delivery and the beauty of the child. Mary wrote at once to Lord Byron, giving him the news, and, a few days later, Shelley wrote to him also, describing the baby as a "creature of exquisite symmetry."

Another bright spot in this harrowing month was Leigh Hunt's publication of Shelley's *Hymn to Intellectual Beauty* in his paper *The Examiner*. At Shelley's special request it was published anonymously, however, for Shelley believed that his unpopularity with critics and reviewers would make a fair judgment of his work impossible. In fact, it received very little notice of any kind.

January 24, the day of the court hearing, was also small William's first birthday, and Mary recorded in her diary the hopeful wish that "my William's star may be a fortunate one to rule the decision of this day." In the next entry, however, she wrote, "I receive bad news and determine to go up to London." The news was that Lord Eldon, the Chancellor, had decided to review the case himself in private hearings—a proceeding which Shelley's lawyers told him boded very ill for his cause.

The case dragged on for weeks, and during the first part of it the Shelleys stayed in Hampstead with Leigh Hunt, welcomed by his wife, Marianne, and their many small children. Hunt's frank, warmhearted sympathy was a special boon to the harassed Shelleys. The household was happy if noisy, for the Hunts had interesting and novel theories about the upbringing of children. Their offspring were never punished or even scolded. Instead they were allowed unrestricted freedom until they were old enough to be reasoned with. After that, argument and logic were supposed to prevail.

At Hunt's hospitable table the Shelleys made many new acquaintances. Among them was Horace Smith, a wealthy businessman who wrote verses and plays and who described Shelley vividly at this time as "a fair, freckled, blue-eyed, light-haired, delicate-looking person whose countenance was serious and thoughtful; whose stature would have been tall had he carried himself upright; whose earnest voice, although never loud, was somewhat unmusical . . . it was impossible to doubt, even for a moment, that you were gazing upon a *gentleman,* a first impression which subsequent observation never failed to confirm, even in the most exalted acceptance of the term, as indicating one that is gentle, generous, accomplished and brave."

Frail young John Keats was often there too, as were Hazlitt and the painter Benjamin Haydon, with whom Shelley had many lively arguments over religion. By the end of February, Albion House was ready at last and the Shelleys moved into it. Claire soon joined them, bringing her baby, who now, at Byron's wish, was renamed Allegra. With Elise, a second nursemaid named Milly, a cook, and a gardener, their household seemed complete and Mary looked about her thankfully. "This will be our home forever," she declared. "Mrs. Shelley of Albion House," she added. "How settled, how comfortable that sounds after all our wanderings!"

Albion House was a large, rambling, Gothic-style structure with pointed windows and pseudo battlements surrounded by four acres of low-lying meadow land. Shelley quickly selected one huge, high-ceilinged room for his library and decorated it with plaster casts of Greek gods and goddesses. Never before had they had so much space at their disposal, and they immediately invited all their friends for a stay with them. To Mary's delight, Godwin himself came for a time, as did Horace Smith and the whole Hunt family. Peacock, who lived nearby, was a constant caller, and William Baxter, in whose home Mary had lived in Scotland, visited them in September.

Peacock and Shelley took many long walks from Marlow out over the surrounding countryside. On one occasion they went by foot as far as London, a distance of thirty-two miles. They also spent long hours on the water, for, as soon as they arrived, Shelley had got himself a boat, which he named *The Vaga*. "The Vaga*bond* would be a better name for it," Peacock suggested with a grin, and promptly wrote the extra syllable on the vessel's prow with a piece of chalk.

The Hunts' eldest boy, seven-year-old Thornton, wrote afterward of his pleasure in Shelley's company. "I went with him rather than with my father, because he walked faster and talked with me while he walked, instead of being lost in his own thoughts. . . . a love of wandering seemed to possess him in the most literal sense; his rambles appeared to be without design, or any limit except my fatigue; and when I was 'done up' he carried me home in his arms, on his shoulder, or pickback."

In spite of the warnings given Shelley by his lawyers, Lord Eldon's decision, delivered on March 27, came to him as a crushing surprise. Shelley was denied custody of his children. They were made Wards in Chancery and the Lord Chancellor would select a guardian for them and make all the arrangements for their education. Although the case was supposed to be heard in private, newspaper reporters had gleaned enough of it to seize upon what facts they could find and inflate them unmercifully. Shelley was portrayed as a monster of vice and iniquity, and his cherished beliefs were held up to scorn and, even worse for him to endure, to vicious satire and ridicule.

Shelley's wound was deep. For a time Mary feared that he would be completely destroyed, that he could not survive. With all her love and loyalty she sprang to his defense. Shelley's impassioned version of the controversy seemed to her the most sacred truth: his enemies must therefore all be despicable liars.

She was to learn now, however, that, for all his sensitivity, deep within him lay a core of tough and stubborn confidence in his own integrity. This had steeled him before, and after the first shattering impact he was able to turn his mind to new projects—it seemed almost to stimulate him. Mary herself took the blow hard also, for she was pregnant again. She was also discovering that managing so large an establishment was a difficult task, one for which

she had neither liking nor talent. Their own simple vege-
tarian meals and Spartan manner of living required little
planning, but providing for so many guests was a different
matter.

Besides all this, Claire and Allegra's presence with the
Shelleys was causing gossip in the neighborhood. Their
efforts to shield Claire from public disgrace by explaining
that Allegra was "the child of an invalid friend" were being
greeted with lifted eyebrows and knowing smiles. Soon
it was even whispered about that Shelley was the child's
father—an insinuation which Mary simply could not
endure.

Mary therefore added her plea to Claire's frantic urging
and Shelley wrote again to Lord Byron. He explained the
matter to him and asked that Byron make provision for the
care of his daughter so that she would no longer be
Shelley's responsibility and need not live here in his
family. Byron's replies from Italy, where he was now estab-
lished, were vague and evasive. It was soon clear that he
would do nothing at all for Allegra at this distance. Byron
would not interest himself in Allegra until he saw her for
himself, he wrote Shelley, and he refused absolutely to
allow Claire to bring her: if *she* came, he would receive
neither her nor Allegra. They must find someone to take
the child to Byron. Mary found the solution to their problem: they would take Allegra to Italy themselves.

They talked this over eagerly and at length. The more
they discussed it, the better the plan seemed. It would
solve not only the problem of Allegra but others as well.

They were learning, too late, that Albion House, which had seemed so perfect, was hopelessly damp and drafty, even in warm weather. "All the books in the library are mildewed," Mary had written to William Baxter. With Shelley's weak lungs, the prospect of spending an English winter here was frightening. Italy was the place for him— for all of them!

There was still another reason why Mary wished to leave England. Shelley had once expressed the belief that since the vindictive Lord Eldon had deprived him of Ianthe and Charles, he would not be satisfied until he took away their adored William also. Once implanted, that fear had grown into an obsession in Mary's mind. It haunted her sleep and brought frequent nightmares, from which she awoke cold with panic.

They would have to wait, of course, until after the final settlement of the Chancery case and also until the birth of Mary's child, which would be early in September. To make things more complicated, in his first enthusiasm Shelley had signed a twenty-one-year lease on Albion House and that lease would have to be sold before they could get away.

During these turbulent months Mary had somehow managed to finish the manuscript of *Frankenstein,* and late in May she and Shelley went to London to try to arrange for its publication. John Murray turned it down promptly and, while waiting to hear from Ollier, another publisher, Mary stayed at Skinner Street. Suddenly remembering that he had invited all the Hunts for a three-week visit,

Shelley hurried back to Marlow. He was also anxious to resume work on a long poem whose title he had changed from *Laon and Cythna* to *The Revolt of Islam*. He had dedicated the work to Mary in verses beginning:

> So now my summer's task is ended, Mary,
> And I return to thee, mine own heart's home.

In it, too, he paid tribute not only to Mary herself but also to Mary Wollstonecraft and William Godwin, her parents.

Besides his writing, his studies, and the entertainment of his guests, Shelley was now involved in trying to help the poor cottagers of the district. Like all the harshly downtrodden workers of those days, they were suffering extra hardship from the ruinous aftermath of the Napoleonic Wars. Shelley had once aspired to become a physician and had studied medicine for a short time. He used this knowledge in visiting the sick, but he handed out nourishing broth and small coins to his patients instead of trying to dose them. He also distributed warm blankets, and when Peacock cynically remarked that these would probably all be sold for gin, Shelley was practical enough to have them stenciled with his name in large black letters.

In the meantime he entered the controversy over political reform which was sweeping England by writing a tract entitled *A Proposal for Putting Reform to the Vote, Throughout the Kingdom,* which Ollier published under the authorship of "The Hermit of Marlow."

Ollier had shown no interest in *Frankenstein,* and

Mary returned, disappointed, to Albion House to wait through the rest of the summer for the birth of her child. She spent what hours she had free from household cares on her studies and in finishing the *Journal of a Six Weeks' Tour,* in which she described their travels on the Continent during the idyllic time of their elopement.

Willmouse was thriving. He had learned to walk and Shelley wrote to Hogg of his son's progress. "He has become metamorphosed since you were here into a featherless biped; he lives and inhabits his father's house but he has ceased to creep. He walks with great alacrity."

Everyone agreed that he was an enchanting child—rosy, blue-eyed, sweet-tempered—and the fear that Lord Eldon might one day decide to take him away from her was a constant torture to Mary. On September 2 her new baby was born, a little girl, whom they named Clara Everina. Mary's recovery was slow, for the household was far from restful. Guests were as numerous as ever and she had to cope with them all herself, for Shelley had had to go up to London again soon after the baby arrived. The charming Hunts had proved to be greatly in need of money and, along with Godwin, Claire, and Charles Clairmont, Shelley generously added them to those whom he was supporting. The result was that he now found himself in difficult financial straits. He was, in fact, arrested for debt on October 20 and spent several days in jail before his lawyers extricated him. They did so by selling off part of an inheritance from his grandfather which they had been holding for him in hopes of later getting a better price for it.

One of the letters Mary sent to him in London reflected her low spirits at this time. She told him plaintively of how the Hunts had set off for a walk without waiting for her, although they knew that she wanted to go and was still too weak to venture out alone. "Peacock dines here every day *uninvited*, to drink his bottle," she added. "He is very ill-tempered toward the Hunts, or so they complain to me."

A letter sent soon afterward was more cheerful. It dealt with further reasons for them to leave England for Italy, which would surely solve all their problems. "Willy kisses the paper to say good-night to you. Clara is asleep," she ended.

Shelley was in the city again in late November to make some revisions which Ollier had insisted upon in his poem *The Revolt of Islam.* Mary joined him there, pleased in the expectation of seeing her girlhood friend Isabella Baxter, who was then staying in London. Isabella was now married, however, and her husband, a Mr. Booth, was a man of rigidly orthodox opinions. Shelley's published views on religion so outraged him that he forbade his wife to have anything to do with either of the notorious Shelleys and even pressured his father-in-law, good-natured William Baxter, to break off his friendship with them.

This was a cruel disappointment to Mary. Her holiday in London was further darkened when Shelley's physician gave the opinion that Shelley was positively menaced by consumption. This news forced a decision upon them at last. By December they had made up their minds that they must at all cost leave Albion House and travel to Italy as soon as possible. The matter of a guardian for Ianthe and Charles was still unsettled, but since that was entirely in the hands of the Lord Chancellor, there was little that Shelley himself could do about it. His physical presence was not required: he could give instructions to his lawyers by letter from Italy to handle it for him.

Godwin protested bitterly against their leaving the country until Shelley paid off more of his debts for him. Shelley did this by raising the money on another of the ruinous post-obit loans he had used before. Then the new year of 1818 arrived, and, in January, Shelley finally found a publisher, Lackington and Hughes, for Mary's novel, *Frankenstein*. A short time later, by means of an advertisement in the *Times,* he succeeded in selling the lease to Albion House.

At last life seemed to be dealing more kindly with the Shelleys. They were both in high spirits when they left Marlow on February 7 and moved to London in preparation for their travels to Italy. Their rooms were on Great Russell Street, Covent Garden, near where Charles and Mary Lamb were then living. There they gathered their friends about them and enjoyed evenings of talk with Hunt, Hogg, Peacock, Horace Smith, and Keats. They also attended the theater and the opera. Seeing them in a box at a performance of Mozart's *Figaro,* Hunt described Shelley as "a thin, patrician-looking cosmopolite" and commented on the whiteness of Mary's shoulders above her crimson velvet gown.

On March 9, the day before they were to sail, they took the three children—William, Allegra, and Clara—to the church of St. Giles-in-the-Fields and had them baptized in the Christian faith. This, like their marriage ceremony, was not an act of piety, the Shelleys assured each other. It was rather a precaution against possible official interference in the children's future. That evening the Hunts came for a final farewell. Thoroughly exhausted, Shelley fell asleep in his chair before they left, and they tiptoed out without waking him to say goodbye.

March 10 was their last day in London. They took a coach in the early dawn, breakfasted in Dartford, reached Dover in the evening, spent the night there, and shipped out for Calais in the morning. The voyage was stormy, but for once Mary was so happy and relieved to be escaping from England and its many problems that she actually enjoyed it.

On French soil at last, Shelley engaged a large coach to carry them southward. "We shall be traveling into the spring," he said.

CHAPTER NINE
1818

Although the coach was large and roomy, three babies, two nursemaids, Claire, Mary, and Shelley with all their baggage made a full load. The French roads were the best in Europe, thanks to Napoleon, but even so they were dusty and often rough. At Mâcon the incessant jolting broke one of the coach's springs, and the party was delayed while it was repaired by the local blacksmith.

Claire was gloomy and snappish and all the babies soon grew fretful. In spite of every discomfort, however, Mary's spirits were still high, for it seemed to her that Shelley's health had already begun to improve in the fine, sunny weather. That alone would have been enough to account for her elation, but to add to it she felt a heady sense of release, of freedom from her former haunting dread that the Chancellor might take her children from her. Now they were out of his reach at last!

When Shelley and Mary were not admiring the fine, fertile spring countryside through which they rode, they were reading or eagerly discussing what they had read—a book of lectures by Schlegel, a French translation of Aristippus, *A Tale of Rosamund Gray* by Charles Lamb, and a new volume of poems by Leigh Hunt entitled *Foliage*. This last Shelley could not bring himself to admire, for all his affection for the writer. Hunt's poetry seemed lifeless and monotonous to him, "as pedantic as though culled word by word from a dictionary."

They reached Lyons on March 21. Walking out in the evening from their inn to view the meeting of the two great rivers, the Rhone and the Saône, they could see in the distance both the Jura Mountains and the Alps. The sight brought back memories of Geneva and Lord Byron, and that night Claire kept them all awake by indulging in one of her fits of hysterical weeping.

They continued on to Pont Beau Vois, where a bridge marked the frontier between France and the territory of Savoy, then under Sardinian rule. Customs agents went through their luggage and discovered that some of Shelley's many books were written by Voltaire, others by Rousseau. These radical works were strictly banned by the local government. They would have been confiscated then and there but for the kindly intervention of a high official of the Church of England, a canon who had once met Sir Timothy Shelley at the castle of the Duke of Norfolk. On his request, Shelley was allowed to keep his volumes in an officially sealed package until they had passed through the country.

Their route then led them by way of wild mountain valleys hemmed in by awe-inspiring cliffs. "These rocks cannot be less than a thousand feet in height," Shelley exclaimed, gazing upward. "This whole scene is like that described in the *Prometheus* of Aeschylus." He was later to use the memory of this place in his own *Prometheus Unbound*.

Rain delayed them at Chambéry and they did not reach the foot of the Mont Cenis Pass until March 28. The next morning they started up the steep but well-graded road to the summit. Two days later they dined at the guest house there and blessed Napoleon for building so good a highway over the difficult pass. "Of course it was done to further his schemes of conquest, not because he had any concern for his fellow men," Shelley reminded them. "But happily it can now serve peaceful travelers."

Downward, then, and into Italy at last. At Susa, a city on the banks of the river Dura, they saw a Roman arch of triumph erected centuries before in honor of Augustus Caesar. It stood in lonely splendor on a spring-green lawn overgrown with violets and primroses. Mary trailed her long skirts through the dewy grass, gathered handfuls of the blossoms, and buried her face blissfully in their fragrance. "Surely Italy has been rightly called 'a foretaste of Paradise'!" she exclaimed. "We can continue our lives here in happy peace."

Shelley had written several letters along the way to Lord Byron, who was then in Venice, announcing their arrival with Allegra. Disappointingly, when they reached Milan on April 4 they found no answer whatever from him. Claire was frightened and angry, and Mary too felt alarmed misgivings. Would their whole journey be in vain?

Shelley, however, was supremely confident that his plan would work out and refused to worry. He and Mary therefore left Claire in Milan in charge of the nurses and children while they set off together to Lake Como hoping to find a house for them all. The far-famed beauties of Como enchanted them both and, after looking about, they made an offer for a magnificent, partially ruined estate, the Villa Pliniana, said to have been founded by the Roman writer Pliny. Years later Mary was to depict this place in her novel *The Last Man*.

They returned to Milan to wait while their negotiations for the villa went forward and, on April 13, when they still had not heard from Byron, Shelley wrote to him again. In this letter he described their prospective home in glowing terms and invited Byron to join them there for a visit. On leaving he would of course take Allegra back with him to Venice.

Byron replied at last, and from his letter the Shelleys learned for the first time that Claire herself had written to him several times while they were gone—something she had promised not to do. Claire's vanity still would not allow her to believe how much her former lover now truly detested her. Byron's reaction was swift and harsh. He addressed himself to Shelley and stated that he wanted nothing whatever to do with Claire. He would neither see her nor accept letters from her—he had told her that before and now he repeated it. If he took Allegra it must be with the understanding that Claire's parting with her child would be final. She must agree, and in writing, never to see her again!

In the meantime stories had reached Milan of the wild and disreputable life Byron was leading in Venice, and both Shelley and Mary urged Claire not to agree to his terms. Claire thereupon flew into one of her tempers, screaming at them that she would settle her own affairs and that they were interfering inexcusably. "Byron *must* take charge of Allegra and ensure a future for her—perhaps a fortune! That is all that matters," she sobbed.

Against his and Mary's better judgment Shelley then wrote once more to Byron pleading for less cruel treatment, and Byron finally agreed that Claire would be allowed to see her daughter at intervals if she kept away from *him*. Mary then asked that Elise, the Swiss nursemaid who had been with the Shelleys since Geneva, should take Allegra to her father. Elise would remain in Venice in charge of her, so that "the little girl will not suddenly find herself among total strangers," Mary explained.

On April 28 an English messenger named Francis Merryweather, sent by Byron, arrived to escort Elise and small Allegra to the new world that awaited them. They were to go first to the home of the British consul, R. B. Hoppner, who, with his kindly Swiss wife, had agreed to take them in while Byron moved into larger quarters, the Mocenigo Palace. Claire's grief at parting with her child was deep and genuine. Once again Mary was able to forget the trouble her stepsister's misdoings had brought upon them all, and she took her gently into her arms and tried to comfort her.

Meanwhile the deal for the Villa Pliniana had fallen through. Shelley decided that a change of scene—his remedy for most ills—might distract Claire from her misery. The party therefore set off on May 1 for Pisa, arriving there on May 7. That city did not please them, mainly because they were horrified by the sight of so many gangs of convicts chained together in pairs doing heavy, menial work in the streets. They stayed only a few days, then journeyed to the seaport of Leghorn. The attraction for them there was an English lady, a Mrs. Gisborne, who, as Mrs. Reveley, had been a devoted friend of Mary Wollstonecraft's. It was she who had taken the newborn Mary, together with her wet nurse, into her own home at the time of her mother's death. She had kept her there until the bereaved and distracted Godwin could establish a household for little Fanny, Mary, and himself.

Mary had brought with her a letter of introduction from her father, and when she presented it Mrs. Gisborne greeted her with such warmth that they became friends instantly. The lady's second husband, John Gisborne, was a kindly if uninteresting (to the Shelleys) merchant with a prosperous business in Leghorn. Her son by her first marriage, Henry Reveley, was then eighteen and studying engineering.

Mary had hungered all her life for small, intimate details of her mother, details which her austere father had never condescended to give her. Here was an opportunity; she embraced the chance eagerly and spent many happy hours listening to her friend's memories of the lovely and exciting Mary Wollstonecraft.

Mary's father had always stressed his wife's intellectual powers and her independent spirit. Maria Gisborne now told Mary of her mother's warm, impetuous nature and how sensitive and vulnerable she had been to hurt from those she cared for, of the moods of depression which often overwhelmed her. Twice she had attempted to take her own life, Maria Gisborne told Mary. She recalled that Godwin had seemed exactly opposite in temperament to Mary Wollstonecraft, but soon it was clear that her warmth had penetrated his cold, stern logic and he became all that a devoted companion should be.

"When they knew that you were coming they even decided to marry," Mrs. Gisborne recalled, "which was against all his proclaimed principles. I know how truly she enjoyed the new sense of security the marriage brought to her—but for so short a time, alas!"

Young Mary Shelley seemed to her mother's friend to be a happy combination of her parents' natures: a fine, cool, perceptive mind and a loving, loyal heart. Together they sighed again over Fanny's sad fate. "She was a bright and charming little girl," Mrs. Gisborne said. "I loved her dearly. And now here you are, the tiny baby I cared for, with babies of your own!"

Shelley enjoyed talking over engineering problems with Henry, but after a month the heat in Leghorn became too much for him. He found a pleasant house for them, then, on a hill shaded by oak and chestnut trees at the Baths of Lucca, a quiet watering place some twenty miles north of the city. They settled there early in June, and Mary wrote of the place to Maria Gisborne, describing the hot and cold mineral springs in their rustic settings. Of their own house she wrote, "We have a small garden and at the end of it is an arbour of laurel trees, so thick that the sun does not penetrate it. We see fireflies in the evening, somewhat dimmed by the bright rays of the moon. . . . still, we know no one; we speak to one or two people at the Casino, and that is all; we live in our studious way, going on with Tasso, whom I like, but who, now I have read more than half his poems, I do not know that I like half so well as Ariosto. The walks in the woods are delightful. . . . you can either walk by the side of the river or on commodious paths cut in the mountains, and for rambles the woods are intersected by narrow paths in every direction."

Besides the walks and the baths, they enjoyed riding horseback before breakfast, sometimes after dinner. Shelley soon discovered a secluded glen where he often spent the day with his books, bathing naked in the little waterfall when the weather was hot. He had not yet started any new writing but had managed to finish a poem, begun in England, called *Rosalind and Helen,* based on the friendship between Mary and Isabella Baxter. He also spent hours on a translation of Plato's *Symposium,* which he undertook in order to acquaint Mary with the Greek philosopher's thought.

Mary's *Frankenstein* had by now been published and,

although the *Quarterly Review* gave it a scathing criticism, other journals were kinder and its sales were reported to be very good. Mary was pleased, of course, although her own writing seemed to her trivial and unimportant when compared with Shelley's. What really delighted her at this time was that Shelley's health continued to improve and that both her precious children were safely at her side and thriving. Baby Clara was creeping and beginning to stand up, while Willmouse trotted happily among the flowers and chattered away, mixing Italian words freely with his English. They had found, moreover, a clever, active serving man named Paolo, who eagerly assumed most of the household responsibilities, leaving Mary to read and study undisturbed.

The only blot on Mary's bright horizon continued to be Claire. Her sighs and tears for Allegra wakened such sympathy in Mary that they almost dimmed her enjoyment of her own children. Claire soon discovered that the clever Paolo was cheating them in his buying of supplies: Mary must watch him more carefully. And now Claire reported that the letters she had been receiving from Elise had brought alarming news. According to the Swiss nursemaid, life in Byron's Venetian palace was lurid indeed. The place was full of quarrelsome Italian servants and his lordship's equally quarrelsome harem of Italian mistresses, while a regular menagerie of pets occupied the ground floor and added to the general dirt and confusion.

All this brought the usual hysterical outbursts from Claire, who learned in the middle of August that Byron had sent Allegra and Elise to stay once again with the English consul, Hoppner. It seemed that even Byron could see that his present manner of living was not suited to the upbringing of a little girl. He had grown very fond of Allegra in these three months, however. "She is very pretty," he wrote to his sister, Augusta Leigh, in England. "Remarkably intelligent and a great favorite with every-body . . . she has very blue eyes and that singular fore-head, fair, curly hair, and a Devil of a spirit—but that is Papa's."

This arrangement for Allegra did not satisfy Claire at all, and she made such a pitiful case for herself that the chivalrous and softhearted Shelley at last agreed to go in person to Byron and do his best in her behalf. Then noth-ing would content Claire but that she should go along. This seemed disastrous folly to Mary, who protested as vigorously as she knew how. "Claire's presence is sure to infuriate Byron again and undo whatever progress has been made," she argued.

All Mary's logic only succeeded in winning the conces-sion from Claire that she would halt her own journey at Padua and wait there, unknown to Byron, until Shelley had done what he could. Claire promised faithfully to abide by her pledge, but as Mary saw them off on their errand she was full of misgivings. Claire's promises were not to be trusted, as she knew only too well.

When they had gone, with Paolo in attendance, Mary was so beset by loneliness and worry that she wrote to Maria Gisborne inviting her and her family to come to

Lucca for a visit. Before they arrived Mary had received a letter from Shelley which did nothing to ease her anxiety. "In my talks with Byron I plan to give him the impression that Claire is still in Lucca," he wrote. "The worst part of this plan is that it will not succeed." (No, Mary thought, *he's* quite incapable of deceiving anybody.) "And *she* will never be satisfied that all has been done," he added.

A few days later another letter from Shelley told Mary that Claire had indeed gone on to Venice with him instead of remaining in Padua and that she was actually staying with Allegra at the Hoppners'! Maria Gisborne's arrival, bringing her calming affection, was a godsend to Mary at this time and especially so because baby Clara, now almost a year old, was running a slight fever.

"It's just the usual 'summer complaint,' a diarrhea from the hot weather," Maria assured Mary. "Babies hereabouts always have it in the summer. It's nothing to worry about."

Mary had little time to enjoy the Gisbornes' company after that, for an urgent letter from Shelley changed all her plans abruptly. It began pleasantly enough. Shelley had succeeded far better than he had hoped. Byron had invited the Shelleys to occupy his Villa Cappucini at Este for a stay. Claire would be allowed there and Byron would send Allegra for a visit. Byron and he had had some frank and friendly talks, many while riding horseback along the outer beach, the Lido. Byron had read him the Fourth Canto of *Childe Harold,* for which Shelley expressed the most enthusiastic admiration.

What dismayed Mary was that Shelley insisted that she start for Este "at once, and without a moment's delay." He enclosed fifty pounds for her to use on the journey and specific directions for her route and the times for departure and arrival. This haste was essential, Shelley wrote, for Byron must be made to believe that Claire was arriving at Este with Mary and had not been in Venice all this time.

Leave their comfortable house at the Baths of Lucca, make a long, hurried journey in the heat of summer? Mary's heart sank. Besides, Clara was not yet well. Maria Gisborne dismissed her fears, however, and urged her to make the trip.

Mary set out in the hot dawn with Clara, William, and Milly, the young English nursemaid, on the five-day journey. The heat, the dust, and the jolting of the carriage aggravated poor little Clara's condition and, by the time they reached Florence, she was running a high fever. There the travelers were delayed by border officials over some trouble with their passports and a whole extra day was spent in straightening matters out.

When they arrived at Este, Mary was exhausted by the long ordeal and baby Clara was clearly very ill. To Mary's further dismay, Shelley himself was in a highly nervous state, for he was suffering stomach cramps from something he had eaten. After a restless and uncomfortable week in which Clara grew no better, Shelley set off to Padua, where the doctors were supposed to be especially able. He said that Mary should leave William with Claire and Milly and follow him with Clara to Padua as soon as he found a physician whom he considered competent to treat the baby.

Mary waited anxiously for his return, hovering with little rest or sleep over her sick child. When Shelley came back at last, it was to announce that "all the doctors in Padua are hopeless numbskulls. We must take Clara to Venice. There's a man there, a Dr. Aglietti, whom Byron has often recommended. I've sent Paolo out to hire a suitable coach and horses."

"To Venice!" Mary protested. "Oh, not another hot, dusty journey! That's out of the question."

But Shelley had made up his mind, and in his excited, feverish mood there was no disputing his decision. Paolo engaged a coach—after more delay—and Mary, Shelley, and the child were bundled into it. Off they went in the humid September weather over execrable roads toward Venice. There was a border to pass before they reached that city, and when they were halted at the barrier they discovered that Shelley had forgotten to bring their passports.

At first the customs men would not allow them to proceed, but Shelley, driven frantic by his own pain as well as Clara's plight, made such an impassioned plea that the men finally let them through. They were human, and the sight of the baby lying so ill in her young mother's arms touched even their stern, official hearts.

Arrived in Venice at last, they had the problem of engaging a gondola, which delayed them further in reaching their inn. By this time Clara was so limp and weak that, numb with terror, Mary could do nothing but hold her tightly against her breast and gaze helplessly into the pitiful little face. Shelley rushed out to summon Dr. Aglietti, but he was gone so long that in desperation Mary sent a servant from the inn to summon another physician.

The man was gentle as he examined the little form, but his face was very grave. "There is nothing to do now but pray, signora," he told Mary at last. "She still lives, but she is already in the hands of God."

Soon afterward Shelley returned. He reported that Aglietti had been out and could not be located, but he refused to believe the other physician's verdict. Off he dashed again in another attempt to find Aglietti, who now seemed to his frenzied mind to be their only hope. He did not find him this time either, and returned to join Mary in her tragic vigil. Clara Everina Shelley lived only until sunset.

CHAPTER TEN
1818 – 1819

After the first searing realization of their loss, Mary saw to her horror that Shelley had all but collapsed from the shock. In panic lest she might lose him too, she somehow crushed down her own emotion to try to comfort him. Thankfully she accepted the Hoppners' invitation to leave their sorrow-haunted lodgings and return home with them. White-faced but outwardly calm, Mary saw her baby buried on September 26 in a cemetery on the Lido.

When Byron called upon the Shelleys soon afterward, his changed appearance startled Mary, for his two years of self-indulgence showed plainly in his face and figure. He was positively stout, his face and hands puffy, and his far-famed "marble-pale" complexion pasty. He greeted her with such gentle kindness, however, that he soon became to her what he had been before—the charming Albé with the magical, musical voice who had fascinated them all on the shores of Lac Leman.

He invited both the Shelleys to the Mocenigo Palace

and there Mary saw what Elise had described, even to the menagerie on the ground floor and at least one of his black-eyed mistresses. With elaborate ceremony Byron introduced the girl as Margarita Cogni, "La Fornarina."

Mary greeted the raffish-looking creature with quiet civility, managing not to show the distaste she felt, for she had caught a well-remembered twist at the corner of Byron's lips. He had teased her often in the past for her "maidenly primness," which he claimed to find very amusing when coupled with Shelley's wild and radical theories and behavior. Now Byron was trying to shock her once again, Mary knew, and she was determined not to give him that satisfaction.

When it was time for them to leave and Byron had bowed over her hand in his familiar courtly fashion, Mary's level gray eyes met his bold gaze steadily. "I have a favor to ask of your lordship," she said.

"Anything, of course," he answered quickly, for he was already half ashamed of his prank.

"When we return to the Villa Cappucini, may we take little Allegra with us for the visit you promised?"

Byron agreed at once. "And will you do me a favor too, Mary? Will you take two of my manuscripts along and copy them out for me in your beautiful, clear hand?"

On September 29, together with little Allegra and the manuscripts of Byron's *Mazeppa* and *Ode to Venice*, they set out on the road they had traveled in such desperate haste before, back to Este. But how sadly different this journey! At the end of it, however, they would rejoin their beloved Willmouse, now twice as precious as ever to them both.

Later, Mary was to describe Este in her novel *Valperga*. "Este is situated nearly at the foot of the Euganean Hills, on a declivity overlooked by an extensive and picturesque castle, beyond which is a convent; the hills rise from behind, from whose heights you discover the vast plain of Lombardy, bounded to the west by the far Apennines of Bologna and to the east by the sea and the towers of Venice."

In a letter to Peacock, Shelley pictured the place in his own way. "At the end of our garden is an extensive Gothic castle, now the habitation of owls and bats, where the Medici family resided before they came to Florence. We see before us the wide, flat plains of Lombardy in which we see the sun and moon rise and set, and the evening star and all the golden magnificence of autumn clouds."

Once settled in such surroundings, the ordeal of their tragedy seemed to have opened up Shelley's imagination into a great gushing out of creativity. The melancholy *Lines Written Among the Euganean Hills* served to purge some of his sorrow. *Julian and Maddalo* described his rides along the Lido with Byron, whom he pictured vividly in the character of Count Maddalo. The magnificent, cosmic drama of *Prometheus Unbound* was begun here. Scarcely noticing those around him, he shut himself up in a small summerhouse and worked all day long, leaving Mary alone with her grief.

With her fears for Shelley eased, the death of her baby struck Mary again with renewed force. A mood of depression settled heavily upon her which she found herself now powerless to combat. Her mind would not function: when she tried to read or to study, her books were mere lines of words that held no meaning. The care of little William might have aided her then, but Claire, thinking to be helpful, had taken the two children off to Padua for a short visit. In desperation Mary turned to the manuscripts Byron had given her and found her one respite in the mechanics of that task. She blessed Albé then for his sensing of her need, but when the work was done she was emptier than before.

It was in this state that Mary wrote a letter to her father, pouring out her heartache to him as she had never dared to do before. His answer was like a blast of cold sleet in her face. "Recollect that it is only persons of a very ordinary sort, and of a very pusillanimous disposition that sink long under a calamity of this nature. We seldom indulge in long depression and mourning except when we think secretly that there is something very refined in it, and that it does us honor," Godwin wrote.

Mary's reaction to this rebuff was to withdraw into herself completely: her sorrow enclosed her in a viselike grip. She walked the echoing halls of the villa and the gardens that overlooked the gloomy ruins of the castle as though in an evil dream—silent, aloof, and cold to all about her. Aloof and cold even to Shelley, for now she was cut off even from him by the torturing realization that he, *he,* whom she had adored and trusted with her whole being, had brought this disaster upon them. *He* had insisted upon the wild journey from Lucca to Venice which had cost the life of her child! Her mind told her that this was true, but her loyal, blindly worshipping heart fought desperately against such an admission. To believe that seemed the basest treachery and the conflict within her was tearing her apart.

Shelley had come to depend upon Mary's unfailing, sympathetic understanding, her praise and support for his every thought and action. Now her withdrawal astonished and bewildered him. He was convinced always of the right-ness and nobility of his motives, and to blame himself for anything was not to be endured. To do so would shatter him utterly. Since his panacea for every ill had now become a change of scene, on November 5 they were on the move once more, with Naples as their destination.

Before they left Este they returned to Venice to put Allegra back in the Hoppners' care and to add Elise again to their party. Both the Shelleys and even Claire were by now convinced that the consul's household was a far better place for the little girl than her father's. Byron's palace, swarming with disreputable hangers-on, had shocked even Shelley, although he still maintained his profound respect for Byron's literary powers. In his *Lines Written Among the Euganean Hills* he had portrayed Byron as "a tempest-cleaving swan" whose writings during his exile in Venice would serve to insure that city's immortality when all else about it was forgotten.

In Ferrara, their first stop, they were delayed by rains. They visited the well-known public library there and were granted a sight of some original manuscripts by Ariosto and Tasso, poets whose work the Shelleys had long admired. On, then, through Bologna and Faenza to Rimini on the Adriatic shore and then by the coast road to Fano. From there the coach trundled them southwestward through the picturesque Apennines, pausing at Spoleto and Terni, where Shelley was enraptured by the Falls of the Verlieno. On November 20 they reached Rome.

The party spent a strenuous week in the Eternal City, for Shelley had developed a veritable fever for sightseeing. Mary went along dutifully and recorded what she saw in her journal, but she was still imprisoned in her strange, remote mood. On one of their rambles in Rome they discovered the quiet little English cemetery near the pyramidal tomb of Cestius, and Shelley described it at length as the most beautiful and solemn place of the sort that he had ever seen, almost as though he were drawn to it by some eerie premonition of the future.

They journeyed on and arrived in Naples on the first day of December. The city on the beautiful, curving bay pleased them all, but even in this warm, bright sunlight the shadow of Clara's death still shrouded Mary's spirits. Shelley found quarters for them overlooking the royal gardens and the sea, and from there they sallied forth every day to see the sights. Hiring a *calesso* drawn by two spirited little black horses, they drove on December 16 to fabled Pompeii, where the amphitheater especially delighted Shelley. Later they made a longer trip to Paestum, where they viewed the great Greek temple.

"I can now understand why the Greeks were such great poets," Shelley commented. "And I can account for the harmony, the unity, the perfection, and the uniform excellence of all their works. Their theaters and temples were open to the sky and the mountains. The flying clouds, the stars, and the deep sky were seen above. They were in perpetual commerce with the harmonies of external nature."

On the way back from Pompeii they stopped to visit a macaroni factory. Shelley greatly enjoyed watching the operation of a lever used in the process, for, ever since his boyhood, machinery had fascinated him. They also made a trip to Baiae and even climbed Vesuvius. Mary and Shelley mounted mules to reach the top, while Claire, who was no rider, was carried up in a sort of sedan chair borne on the shoulders of four men.

After this strenuous exercise Shelley confessed to Mary that a pain in his side which had long plagued him had grown too acute to bear. She found an English doctor to treat him, but the caustic poultice the man applied proved useless and only added to his torment. The next months were unhappy for them all. Claire wept for Allegra while, in the effort to distract Shelley from his physical suffering, Mary stoically suppressed her tears for Clara. In this she met with little success, however, and now it was his turn to withdraw from her. During these months of gloom he wrote *Stanzas Written in Dejection Near Naples* and other, shorter poems so despairing in tone that he kept them hidden from Mary. She found them after his death.

It was during this winter that Shelley was suddenly possessed by one of his wildest and most impractical notions. He decided that all of them, especially Mary, would benefit if he were to adopt a baby girl from a local foundling home to take the place of Clara. He soon discovered, however, that here in Naples there were many legal obstacles in the way of adoption, all the more because Shelley was both a foreigner and a non-Catholic. With characteristic stubbornness he persisted, going to great lengths to circumvent the law, even signing an affidavit that he was the father of the child and Mary its mother. At first he kept the matter hidden from Mary and made arrangements for a Neapolitan family to care for the baby until the Shelleys should be ready to leave Naples. Elena Adelaide, as he named the baby, proved to be sickly and too weak to travel, so that when they finally departed she had to be left behind. Even to this day it is not clear how much of all this Mary and Claire knew.

Next, as if to climax their difficulties, came the revelation that Elise and Paolo had become lovers and that Elise was pregnant. Paolo was willing to marry the girl, he said, but only if Shelley would give him a handsome sum of money for her dowry. Shelley yielded to Mary's plea and to Elise's tears and paid him off, but he also dismissed them both from his service and thereby made a vindictive enemy of Paolo, as time would prove.

Their concern over poor Elise had benefited Mary and

Shelley in one way at least. It had swept away the un-
natural barrier between them and brought them close
again. By late February the pain in Shelley's side had
eased, and he managed to finish the first act of *Prometheus
Unbound*. He then decided to return to Rome, for he had
learned that a lively and cultured group of English people
lived there. Although he himself had no interest whatever
in "drawing-room conversation," he knew that Mary enjoyed and bloomed in congenial society and he hoped that
Rome might cheer her spirits.

They reached Rome early in March and took rooms on
the Corso. Sir William Drummond, a well-known archae-
ologist, promptly called upon them, as did Lord Guilford,
a great traveler and a lover of Greek thought. The Shelleys
were therefore encouraged to believe that they would soon
be a part of a pleasant, stimulating English group.

The two gentlemen had not brought their wives to call,
however, nor did they ever come again. Letters from England had spread the story of the Lord Chancellor's verdict
even here in Rome, while gossip from Venice had revealed
that Shelley was a friend of the notoriously wicked Lord
Byron. The English colony thereupon deliberately and
systematically snubbed the Shelleys. They received no invitations from their countrymen, and if they attended a
soiree in an Italian salon, any other English guests who
were present quickly made their excuses to their hostess
and left.

Mary was so hurt by this ostracism that she lapsed once
more into her cold melancholy. Even Shelley felt the

slights and wrote to Peacock that he was considered "an exile and a pariah . . . a prodigy of crime and pollution, whose look might infect." Most of his concern was for Mary, however, and he finally persuaded her to take up sketching again. For a teacher, he hired a fine Italian artist who was able to rouse her interest in the work. Singing lessons were arranged for Claire. They made a few congenial Italian acquaintances. There was still endless sightseeing to be done and, with more reading and study, their lives began at last to move in a quiet, agreeable routine.

Shelley found a shady and secluded spot in the ruined Baths of Caracalla, a place overgrown with moss and wild flowers, where he could write in peace. Here he finished the next two acts of *Prometheus Unbound* and started a drama based on the tragic story of the Cenci family of Rome. Guido's haunting portrait of Beatrice Cenci had enthralled him ever since he had first seen it in the Colonna Palace.

Without Elise, both Mary and Shelley had now to give more attention to the care of little William, but it was a task they both loved. He was an affectionate, happy child with fair, silky hair and a skin of English cream and roses. His complexion was so radiant that the Italian women who were their neighbors often asked permission to bring in their friends while he was asleep to admire him in his cradle. He chattered equally well in French, English, and Italian, and Shelley began to make great plans for his education.

One day by chance Mary met the Irish artist Amelia

Curran in the Borghese Gardens and discovered that they had been childhood acquaintances. She and Mary still had much in common: Miss Curran gave Mary helpful suggestions for improving her drawing and during that spring she painted portraits of the whole Shelley household, including, of course, William.

Meanwhile the Gisbornes wrote, urging them to return to Leghorn. Mary was now pregnant again, and Dr. Bell, the Scottish surgeon whom she planned to engage for her confinement in November, would be in nearby Pisa at that time. Leghorn was hot in the summer, however, and after much discussion they decided that something similar to the Baths of Lucca, where they had been so comfortable before, would best fit their needs. It was therefore arranged that Maria Gisborne should find and lease a suitable house for the Shelley family in some such location.

Although Dr. Bell had warned Mary that neither Shelley nor William should be subjected to a Roman summer, they waited to hear definite news about their new quarters before setting out. Mary remembered her earlier harrowing journeys and dreaded to begin another long, difficult trip by coach until she was sure that a restful home awaited them at the end of it. They heard from Mrs. Gisborne at last and were preparing to start out when, on June 2, William came down with a high fever.

This second nightmare of tragedy lasted only a few days. "It is the Roman fever," Dr. Bell told the frantic young parents. "A very virulent disease, especially for young children. There seems to be no way of halting it once it attacks."

He applied every remedy in his power while Shelley sat night and day beside his little son's bed, his eyes fixed on the child's face. Claire came to Mary's aid and took turns with her in the nursing, but all their efforts were in vain. William died on June 7 and was buried in the English cemetery which Shelley had praised so highly on their first visit to Rome.

On June 11 they left what had become to them a hateful city and traveled northward to Leghorn. Mary was in a state of almost complete collapse when they reached the apartment Mrs. Gisborne had hastily procured for them near her own home in the city. From there they moved later into more permanent quarters, the Villa Valsovano, a few miles outside the town. Shelley too was exhausted by grief, but, as before, deep emotion served to kindle his creative imagination. As soon as they were settled, he began to work again on his drama of the Cenci, choosing for his study a little tower on top of the building with windows on all sides. When he looked up from a page he could see the Apennines on one side and on the other the sea, with the far, blue islands of Elba and Corsica in the distance.

Mrs. Gisborne was fluent in Spanish, and for diversion Shelley persuaded her to give him lessons in that language. He had heard great things of the Spanish poet and dramatist Calderón, and when he was able to read his works in the original he found them vastly to his own taste, comparable even to Shakespeare. During this time Shelley received by post a copy of Peacock's lately published novel, *Nightmare Abbey*, from its author, with the suggestion that Scythrop Glowry, one of its characters, might be of special interest to him.

Scythrop, in the story, is a young man of good family who had developed a plan for the regeneration of the human species and so of reforming the world. Scythrop had written up his ideas and had them printed, but unfortunately only seven copies of his book had been sold to the public. Shelley read Peacock's kindly satire on himself with great enjoyment and amusement, and he returned, refreshed, to his own writing in what he now called "Scythrop's tower."

Mary had no such outlet for her emotion. Her grief seemed to paralyze her faculties. She was numb and frozen within a private prison of despair, for she blamed no one but herself for William's fate. She was stifled and cut off and unable to communicate with anyone, even with Shelley, in spite of the renewed love between them. What was more, this pregnancy was not proceeding well. She was wretchedly ill most of the time and felt no hope whatever of a happy ending for it. Would not this child be as surely and cruelly snatched from her as the others had been? Or—and this now seemed to her almost a kinder fate—might she not, like her mother, die in childbirth?

CHAPTER ELEVEN
1819 – 1820

Despite her misery Mary tried doggedly to go on with her reading and study, but she was unable to focus her thoughts even upon the novel which had begun to shape itself in her mind. Instead she turned to writing letters, some to Miss Curran in Rome, many more to Marianne Hunt in England. Leigh Hunt usually answered them, for he had formed the habit of writing to the Shelleys every Monday.

"I wish in truth I knew how to amuse you just now and that I were in Italy to try," he told Mary. "I would walk about with Shelley wherever he pleased . . . I should be merry or quiet, chat, read or impudently play and sing to you Italian airs all the evening." He made a special point also of relaying encouraging items to Shelley about how an appreciation of his work had begun to grow in England. Charles Lamb, who, through Godwin's influence, had once declined to meet Shelley, now greatly admired his *Rosalind and Helen*. "Your reputation is certainly rising in your country," Hunt assured him.

The Shelleys went out very little in Leghorn society

during the summer months, but the Gisbornes called almost every evening, and Mary was again able to talk with Maria about her own mother. Now, however, Mary could feel that some strange compulsion always turned their talk toward Mary Wollstonecraft's final days—to her death in childbirth. Mary would catch the look of startled dismay on Maria's kind face as she became suddenly aware of where the conversation was heading, and she noted how hastily her friend would change the subject. Yes, she knows what I am thinking, Mary told herself. And she expects it too.

Shelley was working hard at finishing his drama, *The Cenci,* and at last, in August, he had 250 copies printed in Leghorn, partly because printing was cheap there and partly in order to correct the proofs himself. He had already sent a copy of the play to Peacock, urging him to submit it to Henry Harris of the Drury Lane Theatre, but without Shelley's name attached to it. He wished above all things to have the accomplished actress Eliza O'Neill play the part of Beatrice.

Early in September news reached Italy of the "Manchester Massacre," in which a group of English workers, assembled to hear a speaker, had been fired upon by troops sent to arrest one of their number. Nine people were killed and almost five hundred injured. Shelley was fiercely indignant at the outrage and, in the white heat of anger, he wrote *The Mask of Anarchy*. Although Hunt agreed with Shelley's views, he did not publish it. Shelley had advocated strictly nonviolent resistance. He had even exhorted the people to let the tyrants shed their innocent blood but never to retaliate in kind. Instead, he bade them rely upon superior moral strength to win eventual freedom and victory.

Hunt feared, nevertheless, that the tone of the poem might be misunderstood and that it would injure Shelley's reputation just when it seemed to be gaining some support. He misdoubted especially the effect of the stirring lines

> Rise like lions after slumber
> In unvanquishable number
> Shake your chains to earth like dew
> Which in sleep had fallen on you—
> Ye are many—they are few!

As for *The Cenci*, Harris admired the writing but felt that its subject matter, murder and incest, was too dreadful to present on an English stage. He assured Peacock that, if the author would write another play dealing with a less controversial subject, he would be glad to accept it.

During all this time letters from Godwin had continued to plague the Shelleys. After William's death he had written another unfeeling and critical letter to Mary, chiding her for indulging herself in sorrow "because a child of three years is dead." Shelley himself had protested to Godwin over the tone of that letter and had begged him to write more kindly to his daughter. In answer, Godwin had written back to her that if she expected to stay on good terms with him she *must* induce Shelley to pay her father's debts as he had promised.

This was too much even for Shelley. He sent an indignant refusal to Godwin and wrote also to Leigh Hunt, exposing the whole long and sordid affair. "He heaps upon her misery, stiff misery," he complained, and referred to his famous father-in-law as "this solemn lie; for such, and not a man, is Godwin. I have bought bitter knowledge with 4,700 pounds. I wish it were all yours, now."

On September 4 Charles Clairmont arrived from Spain. He was still a sponge upon Shelley's generosity, but he had developed into a cheerful and interesting conversationalist. His knowledge of Spanish aided Shelley in his study of Calderón, while his presence helped to lift his sister Claire's spirits. She had not heard from either Byron or the Hoppners for months and she was desperately worried about Allegra.

At the end of September the Shelleys moved on to Florence, for their trusted Dr. Bell was to be in that city at the time Mary expected the birth of her child. For Mary's sake they took the journey by easy stages, stopping over a day in Pisa. There they made the acquaintance of Mrs. Mason, the former Lady Mountcashel. One of Mary Wollstonecraft's first positions had been as her beloved governess in Ireland: Mrs. Mason had always kept in touch with her and, after her death, with Godwin. Intelligent, cultured, shrewd, and kind, she proved to be an invaluable friend to the Shelley party. She later referred Shelley to a good doctor who did wonders for his health, she wrote letters to Vienna which enabled Charles Clairmont to get a position there, she befriended Claire in many ways, and she was a staunch and helpful adviser to Mary.

The Shelleys settled into lodgings in Florence early in October in the Palazzo Marini, near the church of Santa Maria Novella. During the warm, bright autumn days Shelley's health began to revive, aided, he felt sure, by the seasonal west wind, "at once mild and animating," as he described it. On one of his many walks through the nearby Cascine wood, the idea for his magnificent *Ode to the West Wind* came to him. He wrote it out swiftly, at the same time finishing the fourth and final act of *Prometheus Unbound*, which he himself considered his finest work, and sent them both off to be published by Ollier in London.

On November 12, 1819, Mary's baby, a little boy, was born after only two hours of labor. Mary's depressed spirits and low vitality had made even Dr. Bell apprehensive for her and the child, but the baby proved to be fine and healthy. They named him Percy and added Florence to his name in honor of the city. "Mary begins to look a little consoled," Shelley wrote happily, while young Percy proceeded to more than double his birth weight in two weeks.

In spite of her baby's blooming health, Mary's past tragedies continued to shadow her mind with dread for his safety. She worried and fretted over his least little ailment and wrote so constantly in this vein to Mrs. Mason that her sensible friend answered at last with a mild reproof. Mary must make an effort to be serene and cheerful while she was nursing little Percy. Otherwise her own morbid mood might upset the child, she warned her.

A little before the baby's arrival, a ward of Shelley's

Uncle Parker had arrived in Florence with her traveling companion. Her name was Sophia Stacey. She was young, pretty, and rich and she was intensely curious about her guardian's nephew, of whom she had heard such intriguing stories. When she met him she was fascinated at once and thereupon took lodgings near the Shelleys in the Palazzo Marini. Shelley was attracted by her fresh, girlish beauty, her appreciation of poetry, and, of course, by her obvious admiration of him. Her gay presence was a welcome contrast to Mary's often querulous state of infirmity and Claire's nagging complaints.

They talked for hours of his family home, Field Place, and its surroundings, and she gave him up-to-date news of his mother and sisters. He showed her about Florence, helped her with her Italian studies, and listened, entranced, while she sang to a harp in the evening. At her request he wrote several new lyrics for her songs, among them the lovely and passionate *Indian Serenade*.

Mary was too weak and too occupied with her baby to share in their expeditions. She could only look wistfully after them as they set off on a day of sightseeing. Claire, sharp-eyed and sharp-tongued, sensed Mary's feeling and did not hesitate to add to her discomfiture with sarcastic comments. She forgot, of course, how often she herself had gallivanted with Shelley in their London days, leaving Mary behind. She was jealous of Sophia's youth and wealth and good looks and, above, all, of Shelley's praise of her singing, which, up to now, had been Claire's private province. Neither Claire nor Mary was sorry when Sophia

and her companion left near the end of December to continue their travels.

Godwin's demands had never diminished. Shelley's indignant letter had had no effect at all upon him and he
continued to write of his needs. His affairs were coming to
a crisis, for he was presently engaged in a lawsuit with his
landlord which could very well ruin him forever. For
Mary's sake Shelley might even now have been willing to
help him, but at this time it was quite out of the question.
His own affairs were in great disorder and he had, besides,
made another commitment.

During the summer Shelley had been immensely excited over news that a ship powered by a steam engine
instead of sails, the *Savannah*, had successfully crossed the
Atlantic Ocean in only twenty-six days! Why could not a
steamship be equally successful in the smaller Mediter-
ranean? He became obsessed with this idea; his imagination soared as he envisioned the project. He easily persuaded young Henry Reveley to build an engine to be
used in a ship and promised that he himself would raise
the money for the enterprise. The steam cylinder and the
pump had been cast on the very day of young Percy's birth.

Since he could not send money to Godwin in England,
Shelley now conceived the idea that the Godwins should
leave that country and its problems and take refuge in
Italy, where living was much cheaper and the climate so
delightful. Godwin could continue his writing and Mary
would have her dearly loved father close at hand. Surely
if they all lived together they could work out their dif-

ferences and misunderstandings by calm reason and logic and so find serenity and peace at last!

The Shelleys discussed this plan for months and even consulted their friends. Mrs. Mason, who knew Godwin well, advised emphatically against it. It would be very difficult, she wrote them, for a man of Godwin's age to change the habits of a lifetime and adapt himself to the absence of long-accustomed trifles. "Philosophy supports in great matters, it seldom vanquishes the small everyday-isms of life," she warned them.

The coming of winter had brought a long spell of chilly rain to Florence, and, even huddled in a fur-lined coat, Shelley suffered from the cold. Dr. Bell advised the milder climate of Pisa, and so, on January 26, the whole Shelley household was once more on the move, this time by boat on the Arno River. In Pisa, Shelley consulted the famous Dr. Vacca, recommended so highly by Mrs. Mason. A sensible, forthright man, Vacca told his patient to throw away all his collection of medicine bottles, take more exercise in the open air, and begin to rely on nature. The doctor was a political and philosophical radical, and this counted so much in his favor that Shelley obeyed his orders and his health began soon to improve.

Mary had not been keeping up her journal for some months, but about the first of January she started it again. "I now begin a new year—may it be a happier one than the last unhappy one," she recorded. It seemed for a time that this hope might be fulfilled. Their quarters were comfortable, lodgings and food were cheap, and for almost the first time they were able to live within their income. Mrs. Mason, taking Claire under her wing, kept her interested and occupied, with the result that she was far easier to live with and less of a drain upon Mary's spirits.

After a frustrating lack of news from Allegra, Claire had learned with some relief that Byron had settled down to a more outwardly decorous life and was now the cavalier of one lady only, a young Italian noblewoman, the Countess Guiccioli. He was proud and fond of Allegra, and the Countess too liked her and treated her kindly. But when Claire had written to ask that Allegra be allowed to visit her again, Byron had refused, through the Hoppners, as always. He did not trust the Shelleys' treatment of children. "Have they ever raised one?" he demanded caustically. He did not want Allegra under their care to "perish of starvation and green fruit, or be taught to believe that there is no deity." He was thinking of placing Allegra in a convent to be educated, he added.

This of course infuriated Claire, who appealed again to Shelley to intercede for her. Shelley wrote a friendly, reasonable letter to Byron in her behalf, but with no success.

By March, Godwin had at last decided that he would not leave England. This was, after all, something of a relief to Mary. Much as she loved her father and loved Shelley, she was clear-eyed enough about them both to foresee many clashes between them if they were under the same roof for any period of time. And as for *Mamma!*

Pisa was now proving to be a very pleasant place to live.

They had made some congenial acquaintances, thanks once again to Mrs. Mason, and Mary had begun to enjoy going out among people once more. She had also taken up working on her novel, which was based on the story of Castruccio, the fourteenth-century Duke of Lucca, and it was later to be published under the title *Valperga*. Her *Frankenstein* had sold so well—better than anything of Shelley's—that her publisher had requested another book from her.

Shelley's *Prometheus Unbound* was now at the printer's in England, and in mid-March *The Cenci* was published. It received a surprising amount of notice, largely unfavorable except in Hunt's *Examiner*. Most of the critics, however, while denouncing Shelley's morals and philosophy, commented upon his remarkable powers as a poet. Some even referred to him as a genius—misguided, but still a genius. Shelley himself was destined never to read many of these criticisms. Since he considered his verse merely a vehicle for the ideas with which he hoped to reform the world, he would have taken very little comfort in being praised for his poetry alone.

In early May the Gisbornes left for a visit to England, and from June 15 to August 15 the Shelleys occupied their house in Leghorn. They went there in order to consult a lawyer who had been recommended by Mr. Gisborne. The villainous Paolo had surfaced again with the threat that if Shelley did not pay him well he would use what he knew of their stay in Naples to blacken his name throughout Italy. Federigo Del Rosso, the lawyer, managed to scare

Paolo into silence, but only temporarily, as the Shelleys were to learn later.

While in Leghorn, Mary and Shelley went late one afternoon for a sunset walk through fields and flower-starred meadows toward the sea. It was a magical evening, one that Mary was to remember forever afterward with wonder and joy. The air was cool and fresh with the scent of a thousand blossoms; the blue-shadowed myrtle hedges were full of fireflies, while the still-bright sky was alive with soaring, singing skylarks. With Shelley's arm around her, her face uplifted to watch and listen, Mary felt the long-lost ecstasy of their first weeks together sweep through her being once again. From this experience Shelley wrote his *Ode to a Skylark,* perhaps his most widely known and best-loved poem.

With the advance of summer Leghorn grew uncomfortably hot and they moved to the Baths of Pisa, about four miles above the city. The garden of their house, the Casa Prinni, reached down to the canal that connected two rivers, the Serchio and the Arno, and the surroundings were delightfully rural and picturesque. Claire did not like the place, however, and in mid-August she returned to Leghorn for a series of visits and for the sea bathing. Claire and Mary had been getting on each other's nerves, and Mary would have been happier if Leghorn had been too far away for Claire to flit back and forth so often. Happier, also, if letters from the Gisbornes in England had not contained such bad tidings of Godwin. The mineral baths had definitely helped Shelley, however, although he was now much depressed by word he had received from Naples. His small "Neapolitan charge," Elena Adelaide, had been ailing most of the year and now news came of her death. It is still a confused mystery how much of this episode Shelley had ever explained to Mary, but she could of course sense his sadness.

Other news from England worried Mary also, but in her turn she did not confide her fears to Shelley. The Gisbornes had written that John Keats was seriously ill with consumption. Shelley had at once written a kind and sympathetic letter to Keats, praising his poem *Endymion* and urging him to come to the mild climate of Italy and to make his home with them. Mary had added her cordial invitation, but her heart was echoing with the warning the doctor had given to Shelley back in England. Shelley had a weakness of the lungs, the doctor had said, and he too was threatened with consumption, the dread malady for which at that time there seemed to be no cure.

Nevertheless, the routine of their lives continued. Reading, study, and writing were interspersed with baths, walks, and often horseback riding along the paths of nearby Monte San Giuliano. Shelley wrote his gracefully light and glittering fantasy, *The Witch of Atlas,* his political satire *Swellfoot,* and the impassioned *Ode to Naples,* while Mary continued with *Valperga.*

By September the Gisbornes had returned to Leghorn, but now there was a distressing coolness between them and the Shelleys. The project of the steamboat had come to an ignominious end, for which Henry Reveley blamed

Shelley's insistence that he build his engine too large to be practicable. Shelley, on the other hand, felt that he had been cheated out of the money he had advanced. Although Mary was completely loyal to Shelley, she was clearheaded enough to see the other side of the question and made the mistake of telling him so. This wounded him deeply: he still had an absolute and passionately held faith in his own rightness and integrity and felt himself cruelly betrayed by her "lack of sympathy and understanding."

September passed. In October, Claire miraculously consented to take a position in the family of a Dr. Botji, in Florence, to teach the Botjis' children. Mrs. Mason had secured the offer of the place for her and, what was more, had persuaded Claire to accept it. In spite of her clashes with Mary, Claire had been quite content to live under the Shelleys' protection. She greatly enjoyed Shelley's stimulating company—was, in fact, half in love with him at times—and she had no taste at all for work of any kind.

Were Percy Florence and Shelley and she really to be alone together at last? Mary hardly dared to believe that such a thing could be possible as she saw him off on October 20 to escort Claire to Florence. Florence, Mary recalled happily, was at least fifty miles away!

CHAPTER TWELVE
1820 – 1821

Shelley returned two days later, but not alone. He brought with him his cousin Tom Medwin, whom he had picked up at Pisa. Mary knew that Medwin had written to Shelley from Geneva and that Shelley had urged him to visit them if he came to Italy. But wasn't he constantly inviting people who had little chance of accepting his invitations? Mary was disappointed to be burdened with another guest, but she managed to conceal her feelings and to welcome Medwin with good grace.

Medwin was a few years older than Shelley. He had befriended him when the two were schoolmates at Sion House before Shelley went on to Eton. Since then Medwin had served for a time in the Army in India. While in Calcutta he had come across Shelley's *Revolt of Islam* in a Parsee bookstall: he had read it first with curiosity, then with interest and admiration. When he reached Geneva, he had therefore got in touch with him. Two of his friends there, he reported, had been equally impressed by Shelley's work and were anxious to make his acquaintance.

"You'll like them both," Medwin assured Shelley. "They're fine fellows and quite as mad about boating as you are. Edward Williams once served in the Navy and Trelawny is a world-traveled seaman and adventurer." Williams and Trelawny! Names that still have a fateful ring when coupled with Shelley's.

Medwin himself had now retired on half pay with the avowed intention of becoming an author. He was amiable, talkative, and rather stupid, but he had boundless confidence in himself. His enthusiasm for Shelley's work endeared him at once to both Shelley and Mary, but soon his long-winded, oft-repeated stories of his life in India began to bore Mary almost to tears.

A week after his arrival torrential rains descended upon them, and the Serchio and their own canal rose and flooded. "Rain all night," Mary wrote in her journal. "The banks of the Serchio break and by dark all the baths are overflowed. Water four feet deep in our house. . . . It was a picturesque sight at night to see the peasants driving their cattle from the plains below to the heights above the baths. A fire was kept up to guide them across the ford; and the forms of the men and the animals showed in dark relief against the red glare of the flame, which was reflected again in the waters that filled the Square."

The next morning the whole Shelley household was forced to abandon its quarters by stepping from an upstairs window into a boat, and in this, at least, Medwin proved himself helpful. Once on dry land they set off by carriage for Pisa, where, on October 29, they took lodgings in the

Palazzo Galetti. Shelley described the place in a letter to Claire, who was still in Florence. Their rooms were on two levels on the south side of the building and they had two fireplaces; the apartment was both commodious and inexpensive. On the upper floor were Medwin's room and Shelley's study, "both delightfully pleasant," he reported. "Congratulate me upon my seclusion. Today I shall be employed in arranging my books and gathering my papers together. Mary has a very good room just below and there is plenty of space for the babe."

On November 5 Medwin came down with an illness which kept him abed for several weeks. He was nursed through it by Shelley. "He administered my medicines, applied my leeches and was assiduous and unremitting in his affectionate care of me," Medwin wrote later. Shelley also read aloud to his cousin, played chess with him, and said kind and tactful things about Medwin's efforts at poetry. He even managed to persuade his own publisher, Ollier, to bring out a volume of it. It was no wonder that in his turn Medwin conceived an enormous liking and admiration for Shelley.

Mary still found their guest excessively tiresome, but he served one useful purpose for her at this time. After he had recovered from his illness he was more than willing to escort her to the parties to which they were now being invited—parties which Shelley always tried to avoid. The Masons had long been popular in Pisa, and now for their sakes the Shelleys were welcomed into their agreeable circle. Shelley shunned most of the salons, but he too enjoyed evenings when a young poet, Tomaso Sgricci, improvised poetic drama on the spot. He was also intrigued by the erratic but brilliantly amusing Professor Francesco Pacchiani, who soon became their most frequent visitor.

In the middle of November, Claire came back to Pisa for a visit. She was uncertain whether or not to resume her work at the Botjis', and Shelley, who missed her lively and admiring—if tempestuous—companionship, urged her to stay. To Mary's great relief Mrs. Mason's good advice once again prevailed. After remaining only a month, partly with the Shelleys, partly with the Masons, Claire returned to Florence.

It was during that month that Professor Pacchiani had been regaling the Shelley household with stories of one of his pupils, a beautiful and talented girl, the daughter of Niccolo Viviani, Governor of Pisa. Her worldly and frivolous mother, jealous for fear the girl's charm and beauty might rival her own attractions, had insisted that Emilia remain in her convent school until arrangements could be made for her marriage. This was taking Viviani a long time because his wife's extravagance had left very little money to use for his daughter's dowry. Emilia had already spent five long years shut up inside the convent.

"She has nothing to hope for in this world," the professor said, "except interminable imprisonment or marriage to whatever stranger her father chooses for her. She is growing truly desperate."

To the daughter of Mary Wollstonecraft, this was of course an unforgivable outrage. She at once obtained a

copy of a Pisan marriage contract, read it over, and discovered that, for a woman, marriage here, as in so many
other countries, was nothing more than a form of slavery.
In a fire of indignation she copied it out in a letter to
Marianne Hunt for her to study and to shudder over also.

On November 29 Mary and Claire went to the convent
with the professor to call upon Emilia. They found her to
be everything that Pacchiani had described. Beautiful, intelligent, sensitive, passionately fond of poetry, she enchanted them both. They returned with such glowing accounts that the next week Shelley and Medwin went with
them to call upon her again.

For the next ten months a flood of warm and affectionate
letters passed between Emilia, the Shelleys, and Claire.
Mary called upon her often, sometimes twice a week, to
bring her books and other gifts. Shelley often went along,
and they spent much time trying to concoct a plan to bring
about Emilia's rescue, but never with any chance of success. Soon the romantic and chivalrous Shelley began to
build the pretty, unfortunate girl into almost a divinity—
an idealized vision, a conception of beauty, love, and perfect, unreserved sympathy in more than human form. The
rapturous outpouring of his poem *Epipsychidion,* written
then, was dedicated expressly to her.

Emilia responded to this kindness and admiration with
pathetic gratitude. Her letters alternated between laments
for her own unhappy captivity and anguish because her
troubles were saddening the lives of her dear friends. Even
after her return to Florence, Claire continued to corre-

spond with Emilia. When Shelley's letters to her began to slacken, however, and she realized that his attention was now centered upon Emilia, she became jealous. Never one to keep her feelings to herself, she began to reproach Shelley and to complain bitterly and sarcastically to Mary.

Mary was none too pleased with the situation herself, for Shelley's open infatuation, a spiritual fantasy though she knew it to be, was causing comment and gossip among their friends. Mary would not admit this to Claire, however: she knew better than to confide to her anything she wished to hide. Instead she kept her own counsel, held her head high, and continued her friendly visits to Emilia, whom she truly liked and pitied.

Another member of their Pisan circle was John Taafe, a genial Irish poet who bore the dubious title of Count. His poetry was banal and commonplace, as were his translations, but he had written an able commentary on Dante which was later published with some success in England. Taafe liked and admired Mary. At one time, to amuse her, he sent her a gift of two furry little guinea pigs with a note that ended, "Oh, that I were one of these guinea pigs, that I might see you this morning!"

Through Pacchiani also, the Shelleys met the exiled Greek Prince Mavrokordatos, a patriot who was deeply involved in plans for the liberation of his country from Turkish rule. He too became a regular visitor, for he and Shelley held many political beliefs in common. Soon he was tutoring Mary in Greek and she him in English. She wrote of this to Maria Gisborne, with whom they were now friendly again. "Do you not envy me my luck that, having begun Greek, an amiable, young, agreeable and learned Greek Prince comes every morning to give me a lesson of an hour and a half?" These lessons continued until the following summer, when the prince left to fight in the Greek war of independence.

In January, Medwin's friend Edward Eleker Williams, his wife Jane, and their baby Edward had arrived in Pisa. Williams, like Medwin now retired from the Army on half pay, was a year younger than Shelley and had been at Eton during Shelley's stay there. He was frank, lively, intelligent, good-humored, a clever painter in water colors, and desirous of becoming a playwright. Both the Shelleys liked him immediately. On his part, two months after his arrival he wrote back to his friend Trelawny his impression of his new acquaintance. "Shelley is certainly a man of the most astonishing genius, in appearance extraordinarily young, of manners mild and amiable, but withal full of life and fun. . . . Lord Byron thinks him by far the most imaginative poet of the day. The style of his lordship's letters to him is quite that of a pupil."

Jane Williams was a very pretty young woman, placid, domestic-minded, and with a lovely singing voice. A second child, a little girl whom they named Rosalind, was born to her about the middle of March, and Jane and Mary had many interests in common in the care of their small children. Shelley at first thought Jane rather empty-headed, but she was a good listener and soon both he and Mary became as fond of her as of her husband. Medwin now divided his company between the Shelleys and the Williamses, which was, of course, a great relief to Mary. Since Ollier had accepted his book of verses, Medwin had become insufferably conceited about his literary gifts and insisted upon reading his efforts to anyone who could be made to listen.

Claire, still in Florence, had seemed to be far more content with her situation than before. Her teaching tasks were easy and she was beginning to enjoy Florentine society. As the spring of 1821 advanced, however, she received news that Byron had followed the Countess Guiccioli to her family's home city of Ravenna and had placed Allegra in a convent school at nearby Bagnacavallo. Claire flew into a fury over this and wrote in great agitation to Shelley, urging him to protest this move to Byron. Shelley did so, but, as usual, received no reply for some time.

In the meantime Shelley had been shocked and saddened to learn that John Keats had come at last to Italy for his health but had come too late: he had died in Rome on February 23. Many people were saying that his death had been hastened by the cruel treatment his poems had received from powerful critics in England. Blazing with indignation, Shelley started the marvelous tribute to Keats's memory which was to be called *Adonais*—"perhaps the least imperfect of my poems," he himself said of it once, with wistful pride.

When this was finished, Shelley was restless for something to do and, with Williams to advise him, procured a small boat which Henry Reveley fitted up with mast, sail, and rudder. Fortunately for them, Reveley went along on their first voyage, a sail on the canal from Leghorn to Pisa by moonlight. For all his experience in the Navy, Williams managed to capsize the craft by standing up suddenly in it when they were halfway there, and Shelley, who could not swim a stroke, had to be rescued and pulled ashore by Reveley. Reveley then took the boat back to Leghorn while the others had to proceed to Pisa on foot, laughing heartily over their mishap. Later, with the boat made safer, they sailed it many times along the Arno and even out to sea.

In May, with the weather growing warm, the Shelleys moved back to the Baths of Pisa for the summer. Shelley usually felt better in hot weather, but this year seemed to be an exception. The death of Keats had reawakened Mary's concern for him, and she wrote in her journal of "a pleasant summer, bright in all but Shelley's health and inconstant spirits; yet he often enjoyed himself greatly and became more and more attached to this part of the country." After the long effort of *Adonais,* Shelley wrote a number of short, vivid verses descriptive of the landscape about them and even a gay and lively one about their little boat.

Mary was still trying spasmodically to finish her novel *Valperga.* The slow progress did not trouble her much. Her own literary efforts never seemed important to her when compared with Shelley's. Even here at the Baths they had a great deal of company. The Williamses lived only four miles away, and they and Medwin were frequent visitors, as were many others of their Pisan friends. The

Gisbornes, who were going back to England for good, came for a three-day stay before leaving, and Claire arrived from Florence on June 29. She visited the Masons in Pisa and the Shelleys at the Baths, but also spent much time in Leghorn for the sea bathing.

Emilia's marriage had now been definitely arranged and she wrote sadly to Shelley, "I beg you to come no more to St. Anna, neither you, nor any of your family. My parents desire that I should henceforth see no one. Every attempt would be vain; we should be humiliated without obtaining anything." All visits to the convent ceased after that.

On August 2 Shelley received a letter from Byron saying that the Countess Guiccioli's father and brother had been expelled from Ravenna for political reasons and that she herself had fled to Florence. She planned to go on to Switzerland, and she was imploring Byron to join her there. Byron therefore urged Shelley to visit him in Ravenna before he left that city.

"But if Byron leaves Ravenna, what is to become of Allegra?" Mary asked in alarm. "You must make sure that he takes her with him or else persuade him to send her to us, to bring up with our Percy. But don't go until after your birthday on the fourth," she added. "I'm planning a surprise for you."

But Shelley, impetuous as ever, set off the next day for Ravenna. Mary soon received a letter from him, a letter containing such horrifying news that she could hardly believe the words on its pages were actually there. Byron had received Shelley cordially, but on the very evening of his arrival Byron had showed him a letter sent by Mr. Hoppner from Venice. In it Hoppner recounted a detailed story which Elise, the Shelleys' former nursemaid, had told to him.

Thwarted by the law from blackmailing Shelley, Paolo, through Elise, was now spreading a tale of how, in Naples, Shelley and Claire had behaved in a scandalous fashion. A child had been born to them there and it had been deposited by them in a foundling home. All the while the two had been abusing Mary, often beating her cruelly.

In his letter Shelley begged Mary to write a denial of all this to Mrs. Hoppner. This she did at once—a long, passionate defense of both Shelley and Claire and a complete refutation of all that Elise had said against them. This was a harrowing experience for both Mary and Shelley, but at least it served the purpose of jarring Mary out of her reserve and bringing them to realize and to appreciate how strong and steadfast the love between them truly was.

Shelley remained with Byron in Ravenna for two more weeks, and during that time their old friendship was warmly revived. Byron's routine was very different from Shelley's, but the younger man adapted himself and the two spent many long night hours talking and, by day, riding together through the pine forests beside the sea. Byron was living a far more regular life now; the Countess had been a good influence on him. He had lost weight and looked far healthier than he had in Venice.

He still had his menagerie of animals. Shelley reported them to Mary as "ten horses, eight enormous dogs, three monkeys, five cats, an eagle, a crow, and a falcon, and all these, except the horses, walk about the house which every now and then resounds with their unarbitrated quarrels . . . I have just met on the grand staircase five peacocks, two guinea hens and an Egyptian crane." There were a couple of fine large geese roaming the premises too, Shelley added. Byron had purchased them the autumn before and had planned to fatten them for his Christmas dinner. He had fed them himself, however, and they had become such pets in the process that he had not had the heart to have them killed, even though he was excessively fond of roast goose.

Byron had reassured him about Allegra, Shelley was glad to write. The Countess was very fond of the child, and Byron himself would never dream of going off to Switzerland and leaving Allegra behind. Byron asked Shelley to visit Allegra at the convent to see for himself how well she was being treated. This he did, taking her a present of a gold chain and a basket of sweets. Taller but as lovely as ever to look at, Allegra was shy at first, but Shelley had a way with children and she was soon won over. Before long they were romping and racing through the convent garden until *he* was exhausted.

Before he left the convent, Shelley asked Allegra what message she wished to send to her mother. "That I want a kiss and a beautiful dress," Allegra told him.

"And what kind of dress?"

"All silk and gold," the child answered.

Some months before this, Byron had expressed the wish

that Leigh Hunt should come to Italy and that he, together with Byron and Shelley, might found a liberal periodical. Byron had long admired Hunt's courageous writings—had, in fact, visited Hunt when he was confined in jail for them. "I'll finance his journey," Byron had said.

Now Shelley reminded him of his suggestion and, although Byron's interest in the project had cooled a little, Shelley's enthusiasm quickly revived it. Byron seemed reluctant to part with any of his own money at this time, however, and Shelley borrowed two hundred pounds on his own bond and wrote happily to Hunt, inviting him to bring his wife and six children and come at once to Italy. Their plans went forward quickly. Byron would move to Pisa instead of Switzerland and Hunt would join them there.

Nothing could have pleased Mary more than this news. She was immensely fond of the Hunts and the prospect of having them nearby delighted her. It more than made up to her for Shelley's absence on his birthday, on which she had planned to surprise him with a portrait of herself done by Ned Williams.

September 8 was the date set for Emilia's marriage, but neither of the Shelleys was invited to any of the festivities. The fever heat in which Shelley had written *Epipsychidion* had been assuaged in the actual writing of it; now Emilia's marriage moved him again to pen several sadly beautiful and haunting lyrics on the subject of lost love.

Five days before her wedding Emilia wrote Shelley another of her fond and pathetic letters, but in this one she asked him to give her a large sum of money. This request from his idealized goddess was a severe shock to Shelley's sensibilities. After *Epipsychidion* had been printed in England, Shelley wrote to ask that it be withdrawn from publication. In one of his letters to Gisborne, he explained why. "I cannot look at it; the person whom it celebrates was a cloud instead of a Juno," he wrote. Thus ended what Mary called, in a letter to Maria Gisborne, "the whole story of Shelley's Italian Platonics."

CHAPTER THIRTEEN
1821 – 1822

The autumn months of 1821 passed pleasantly for the Shelleys at the Baths of Pisa. Mary actually finished *Valperga* at last, copied it out, and sent it off to Ollier in London. During this time also, Shelley's interest in the Greeks' battle for liberty started him on a dramatic poem in their honor to be called *Hellas*. "We are all Greeks, our laws, our literature, our religion, our arts have their roots in Greece," he wrote in the preface to it. He dedicated the work to their friend Prince Mavrokordatos, who was now in the thick of the struggle.

Late in October the Shelleys left the Baths to spend the winter in the city of Pisa. They had found and engaged a handsome, spacious house for Byron, the Casa Lanfranchi on the Lung Arno. For themselves they took more modest apartments just opposite in the Tre Palazzi, while the Williamses settled in another part of the same building. The ground floor of Byron's great palace was to house the Hunts.

After some postponements, the Hunts set sail on November 15, but their ship ran into a storm in the Channel and had to put back into port. That ordeal so terrified Marianne Hunt that she could not be persuaded to embark again until winter had passed. News of this change of plan took a long time to reach Italy, and Mary spent many weeks fitting up the rooms, engaging a cook, and preparing happily to welcome her friends before she learned of their delay.

Byron's cortege of coaches, baggage wagons, servants, and animals finally arrived at the Casa Lanfranchi. To Mary's consternation, Allegra had been left behind in the convent school. Byron had traveled from Ravenna by way of Florence, and as his caravan moved along the road between Florence and Emboli, it met the public coach coming in from Pisa. The vehicles passed close by each other and a pair of dark eyes had peered out at him from a coach window, but Byron had not turned his head to meet their angry gaze. The eyes were Claire Clairmont's: she was on her way back to Florence, and this was the last sight she was ever to have of Lord Byron.

The Countess Guiccioli, together with her father, Count Gamba, and her brother, Pietro, had by this time been ensconced in Pisa for weeks, and Mary Shelley had made a pleasant discovery. "Teresa Guiccioli is a nice, pretty girl without pretensions, good-hearted and amiable," she wrote. With Claire gone, Mary and Teresa soon formed the habit of driving out into the country together almost every afternoon.

To have the Williamses so near was also proving to be a special joy to Mary. Although Jane was by no means intellectual, she was even-tempered and friendly and she and Mary shared many of the same problems in the care of their children and in their housekeeping on very limited budgets. For recreation Jane played the piano and sang, while Mary took up water-color painting with the capable interest of Ned Williams to guide her.

Now installed in his palace, Byron gathered a congenial group of men about him, some of them from Shelley's circle. They must all dine with him once a week, he insisted. They would play billiards or, if the weather were fine, they would all ride out to a special field where he had set up targets and practice pistol shooting with him. For this reason his guests soon named themselves the Pistol Club.

Shelley proved to be a fine shot with a pistol, better, indeed, than Lord Byron, much to that nobleman's surprise. Shelley enjoyed the horseback riding through the countryside and, since he admired Byron's writing so wholeheartedly, he got pleasure from most of his conversation. Byron's worldliness and his ribald humor often offended the sensitive Shelley, however. Since he did not drink, the long hours the other men always spent over their claret bored him and he slipped away whenever he could do so without displeasing his host.

Shelley explained to Mary that he felt himself obliged, even against his will, to keep on good terms with Byron for two reasons. The first, of course, was the everlasting problem of Claire and Allegra. The other, newer reason was the welfare of the Hunts. Shelley sensed that Byron had lost much of his enthusiasm for the liberal journal the three had planned to launch in Pisa. He therefore felt all the more deeply his own responsibility to Hunt, whom he had persuaded to leave his home and travel so far on the promise of Byron's partnership in the venture.

It was at one of his weekly dinners that Byron spoke with irony of how detestably long-lived those persons were from whom one expected to inherit property. "There's my mother-in-law, Lady Noel," he said. "By the terms of my separation settlement a large part of her estate will come to me when she dies. I'll wager you one thousand pounds, Shelley, that she will manage to live longer than your close-fisted father, Sir Timothy."

Shelley agreed good-humoredly, and Byron had the terms of the bet formally witnessed by Williams and Medwin. Only a month later Lady Noel did indeed die, but Byron blandly ignored his wager. Although Medwin and Williams urged Shelley to remind Byron of it, he shook his head and insisted that it be forgotten. "I told you that Byron hates to part with money," he said to Mary, who had herself voiced some indignation over the matter. "The richer he gets, the more he wants to keep all he has." Because Hunt would soon be dependent upon Byron's bounty, this trait of his lordship's had now become a constant, plaguing worry to both the Shelleys.

On another floor of the Tre Palazzi lived an English clergyman, the Reverend Dr. Nott. Byron and Medwin both scoffed at him, saying that he had lost his post as sub-preceptor to Princess Charlotte of England because of some hushed-up scandal. They had also given him the name Slip-knot, because of his skill in evading the bonds of matrimony. Every Sunday, Dr. Nott held religious services for some fifteen or sixteen English residents of Pisa, and when he gave Mary a special invitation to attend, she thought it only neighborly courtesy to accept.

On her appearance in his congregation his sermon turned into a tirade against the sin of atheism and, without actually using his name, it was directed pointedly against Shelley. Offended and embarrassed, Mary wrote a protesting note to the Reverend Doctor, who quickly and fervently denied any intentional slur.

"I could have told you what to expect, Mary," Byron said to her. "Dr. Nott has clearly been revising one of the Ten Commandments to suit his own style. According to him, it now reads: 'Thou shalt, Nott, bear false witness against thy neighbor!' "

In January a new and striking member was added to the Shelley-Byron circle. Edward John Trelawny, the friend of Medwin and Williams, had come from Geneva to Italy with the stated intention of taking a hunting trip into the marshy wilderness called the Maremma, in Tuscany. He hoped to persuade Williams to join him and a friend, Captain Roberts, on the expedition, but he had another motive also. His interest in Shelley and Byron had been roused by Medwin's and Williams's accounts and he was eager to meet the two poets.

Tall, muscular, vigorous, gray-eyed, raven-haired, his

skin browned almost to Moorish hue by tropic suns, Trelawny was a Cornishman of good family with enough of
an income to make him independent. He had an insatiable
thirst for adventure by land and sea as well as an ability to
describe those adventures in vivid and colorful detail.

He arrived in Pisa late one evening, put his horse up at
an inn, ate his dinner, and then called upon the Williamses. They received him joyfully, and all three were
deep in conversation when Trelawny noticed the outline
of a figure in the dark passage just beyond the door.

Seeing the direction of Trelawny's glance, Jane Williams called out, "Come in, Shelley, it's only our friend
Tre, just arrived."

To quote Trelawny: "Swiftly gliding in, blushing like a
girl, a tall, thin stripling held out both his hands; and although I could hardly believe as I looked into his flushed,
feminine and artless face that it could be the Poet, I returned his warm pressure. After the ordinary greetings and
courtesies he sat down and listened. I was silent from
astonishment; was it possible that this mild-mannered,
beardless boy could be the veritable monster at war
with the world—excommunicated by the Fathers of the
Church, deprived of his civil rights by the fiat of a grim
Lord Chancellor, discarded by every member of his
family, and denounced by the rival sages of literature as
the founder of the Satanic school? I could not believe it;
it must be a hoax. He was habited like a boy, in a black
jacket and trousers, which he seemed to have outgrown."

After some conversation, Shelley translated for the group a few passages from the Spanish of Calderón which had especially intrigued him and then he quietly left. "Where is he?" Trelawny asked, looking about the room in surprise.

"Who? Shelley? Oh, he comes and goes like a spirit, no one knows where," Jane Williams answered, smiling.

A few minutes later Shelley appeared again, this time bringing Mary along to meet the newcomer, and Trelawny later recorded a description of Mary too. After commenting on her parentage as "a rare pedigree of genius," he wrote, "The most striking feature of her face was her calm gray eyes: she was rather under the English standard of a woman's height, very fair and light-haired." With unusual and sympathetic perception he noted also that she was "witty and social and animated in the society of friends, though mournful in solitude; like Shelley, though in minor degree, she had the power of expressing her thoughts in varied and appropriate words."

Trelawny's coming was like a fresh, blustery sea wind blowing through their select little group of expatriates. It was plain that he liked and admired Shelley from their first meeting, and his affection for him never wavered. He enjoyed Byron too, but he found his lordship's mordant, cynical wit far inferior to Shelley's noble, idealistic sincerity.

As an experienced seaman, he showed much interest in the little flat-bottomed boat that Shelley and Williams used on the Arno, but he suggested that they ought to have a better one. His friend, Captain Roberts of Genoa, could build a fine, seaworthy little vessel, just the thing for them, he declared.

Shelley and Williams both took fire at the idea, and when Trelawny brought them the model of an American schooner which he favored, they urged him to engage Captain Roberts to build a thirty-foot undecked boat for them on the same lines. Nothing else was talked about for weeks, although neither Mary nor Jane Williams favored the idea at all.

No sooner had Byron heard of their project than he too had to have a boat of his own built by Captain Roberts: his must, of course, be far larger and more elaborate. The plans went forward with innumerable discussions and with some changes. Williams had a pet idea of his own and, although both Trelawny and Roberts pointed out serious and even dangerous flaws in it, Williams managed to bring Shelley to his way of thinking. Since Shelley was, as usual, paying for the whole project, Williams's design was adopted.

One day, watching Trelawny swimming and diving with great enjoyment in a deep pool of the river, Shelley decided that he too should learn to swim. "I'll give you a lesson," Trelawny offered.

Shelley thereupon shed his clothes and jumped in. He sank like a stone, seemed to make no effort to rise to the surface, but, instead, lay quietly on the bottom of the pool "like a conger eel," as Trelawny later described it. Shelley would have drowned then and there if Trelawny had not plunged in and hauled him out.

Shelley seemed amazingly unperturbed by his narrow escape. "I always find my way to the bottom of a well," he told Trelawny. "They say that Truth lies there. In another minute I should have found it, and you would have found an empty shell. It is an easy way to get rid of the body." Trelawny was far more shaken than Shelley by the experience and he did not offer again to teach him to swim.

At first sight of the Cornishman, Byron had been struck by the man's resemblance to Othello. Now he suggested that their group put on the play together. Trelawny should be Othello; Byron, Iago; Medwin, Roderigo; and Williams, Cassio. Mary was cast as Desdemona and Jane as Emilia. In contrast with their Geneva days, Byron's festivities in Pisa had heretofore been strictly stag affairs, and Mary welcomed this chance to have a part in them again. They held several rehearsals, and it was plain to everyone that Byron's expressive face and voice were those of a superb actor.

Shelley had not been given a part. "You're far too honest to be an actor," Byron had told him. Nor had Teresa Guiccioli, for she could not speak English. Perhaps for this reason she soon managed to persuade Byron that gentlefolk in Italy never engaged in such affairs as private theatricals; they would therefore be viewed as vulgar and undignified by Pisan society. The whole thing was then abandoned.

The early Italian spring advanced, bringing warm winds and burgeoning flowers. In a letter to Marianne Hunt, still back in England, Mary described how she and Jane had been trying to reach some violets growing in a deep ditch when a rough-appearing countryman came by and insisted upon picking them for them. He handed a great bunch to each lady with a bow and a smile. He would accept no money; "I did it for pleasure," he assured them.

In this lovely climate March was as balmy as May in England, and Mary felt herself growing younger, she wrote. Percy was thriving. Shelley, happily absorbed in the building of his boat, was also producing a series of lovely lyrics. Pretty, sweet-tempered Jane entertained them almost every evening by singing and, because their piano was so bad, Shelley had bought a guitar for her. Mary longed for the day when the Hunts would join them and Jane and Leigh Hunt could sing duets together.

Mary had seldom been so happy as she was this spring, and yet—and yet. After all the disasters that had befallen her, she could not quite trust this seeming security. Often, when she found herself alone, her melancholy moods returned and with them a sense of dark foreboding in spite of her efforts to reason it away.

It was Claire, of course, who shattered Mary's fragile interlude of peace. Claire had been writing to Byron again. Frantic over thoughts of Allegra in that faraway convent, she had persuaded Mr. Mason to make a secret visit there. His report was not good. The place was damp, chilly, and unhealthy; there had been no fires in the students' rooms even in winter. When her complaining letters to Byron were not answered (as they never were), she turned to Shelley and begged him to intercede once more for her with his lordship.

Shelley was away when her letter came. He had gone off house-hunting with Ned Williams, for they had decided to find a place for the summer near the shore where they could sail their new boat. Claire's agitated missive was waiting for him when he returned and, against his better judgment, he made one more effort on her behalf. He only succeeded in angering Byron, who declared that Shelley was interfering inexcusably in his affairs. He refused outright to discuss the matter of Claire and Allegra with him ever again.

At this news Claire lost her head completely. She wrote to Shelley that she was planning to kidnap Allegra and spirit her out of the country, and she demanded that he help her in this mad scheme. The Masons were encouraging her in this, she assured him, as was their former nursemaid, Elise. The girl had turned up in Florence and was now denying that she had ever told any scandalous stories to the Hoppners.

The idea of kidnapping a child from an Italian convent was too harebrained even for Shelley. He wrote a series of urgent letters to Claire, trying to dissuade her and bring her to reason. He would have nothing to do with such a foredoomed plan, he told her. Moreover, if she went ahead with it herself, Byron would never believe that he had not had a hand in it. He would undoubtedly challenge Shelley to a duel, which Shelley could not possibly refuse, and disaster would inevitably follow for them all. Claire finally promised to give the matter up, but not until both Mary and Shelley had been deeply shaken.

A letter from England soon after this brought the news that Ollier had turned down the manuscript of Mary's new novel. She wrote back to Godwin, asking him to try to find a publisher for it, with the understanding that he could keep whatever money it brought. Even though her own writing seemed unimportant to her, it was a disappointment and, together with the knowledge that she was now pregnant again, it added to the nervous unrest and near-exhaustion that Claire's antics had brought upon her.

Then, on March 24, the members of Byron's Pistol Club had a brush with violence, almost with death, as they were returning from one of their evening rides together. Byron, Shelley, Trelawny, Count Gamba, Count Taafe, and a Captain Hay were riding ahead while Teresa and Mary, in the Countess's carriage, followed some distance behind to avoid the horsemen's dust. As they drew near the city gate a mounted dragoon came dashing up from behind through the group of riders and jostled Count Taafe as he passed. "Shall we endure this man's insolence?" the Irishman called out.

"No!" Byron answered. "We'll bring him to account." He spurred after the cavalryman, with all the rest of the party following except for the suddenly prudent Taafe. When they overtook the dragoon, a sergeant-major named Masi, he proved to be half drunk, and when they demanded an explanation of his behavior, he cursed them and threatened to arrest them all.

Byron laughed in his face. "Arrest indeed!" he said, and rode on through the city gate with Count Gamba toward Byron's house, where they meant to arm themselves and return. When the others tried to ride after him, Masi wheeled his horse across the gateway, drew his saber, and swung it wildly at the foremost of them, who happened to be Shelley.

Shelley ducked and avoided the blade, but the hilt struck him. It knocked him from his horse, while Captain Hay, trying to shield Shelley with his riding cane from further blows, received a slash across his face. Masi flourished his saber about wildly a few more times, then rode on into the city.

There he met Byron and Count Gamba returning to the fray. Byron was now armed with a drawn sword stick. After some argument, the man finally gave his name and rank and then went galloping off again into the dusk. As he passed Byron's house, one of his servants, convinced that this man had attacked his master and perhaps killed him, rushed out, thrust at him with a pitchfork, and stabbed him in the stomach.

Shelley was stunned and dizzy and Captain Hay was bleeding when the carriage with the two ladies arrived on the scene. Teresa promptly fainted. All was confusion, as everyone tried to explain what had happened, and a hostile crowd began to gather. The most serious news was that the dragoon had been taken to the hospital and that his wound might well be mortal.

Masi lingered between life and death for some weeks, while the Pisan authorities tried to sift through the conflicting evidence and find out who had wounded him. The dragoon recovered at last, but the two of Byron's servants who were suspected of the attack had been kept in jail the whole time and one of them was finally banished from Pisan territory. What was more, the Gambas, exiled from their home in Ravenna because of their liberal activities, were now in the disfavor of the Pisan regime as well.

Meanwhile, Shelley and Williams had arranged to rent two pleasant houses at Spezia on the coast. On April 15, perhaps because of the Masi incident, they received word that neither of those places was available after all. Mary, already ailing from her pregnancy, could not help feeling some relief at this news. She dreaded the task of moving, of leaving their comfortable quarters in Pisa. Dr. Bell had advised her, moreover, to remain as quiet and tranquil as possible during these last months before the birth of her child. The good doctor had spoken gravely when he gave her this warning, and she knew that her condition was giving him some anxiety.

When a letter from Claire arrived, Mary opened it with dread. What was she demanding now? It was not a demand this time, however, but an announcement. She was to have a vacation, she wrote, and she would arrive to join them in a few days.

Claire in Pisa, on the same street and almost opposite Lord Byron! Mary knew that in Claire's present state of mind she was capable of any rashness. There was no time to stop her, however: she arrived, and after a nerve-strained week in which Mary somehow managed to keep her out of sight and away from Byron, practical-minded Jane Williams thought of a solution to their dilemma. "Ned and I will take her with us to Spezia on another house-hunting trip," she offered.

The Williamses bundled her off on April 23, and Mary and Shelley breathed sighs of relief as the party disappeared. Still another crisis with the temperamental Claire had been avoided! They had barely time to express these emotions to each other when a servant came hurrying across from Byron's palace bringing a message from his master. Would Shelley come to him at once? It was urgent.

Shelley returned, pale, shaken, and with dreadful news. An epidemic of typhus fever had swept through Allegra's convent. The little girl had died of it on April 19.

CHAPTER FOURTEEN
1822

For a moment Mary could only look up into Shelley's face while it wavered before her eyes, then faded away into a white mist. She reached dizzily for support and felt his arms encircle her. "Dead?" she echoed. "Allegra dead? No, it *can't* be true!"

But it was only too true, he told her brokenly. Allegra had been ill for some time, it seemed. Byron had known of it, and he had been concerned enough to send two of the finest available doctors to treat her. At first her malady had been wrongly diagnosed as a consumptive fever. According to the best medical practice of the day, she had been bled for that several times and had seemed to be making a good recovery. Then she had taken a sudden, fatal turn, and after that, for all their skill, they could not save her. Byron had been prostrate with grief.

"And Claire!" Mary whispered. "Oh, poor, poor Claire!"

They stared at each other, the same thought in both their minds. Claire must be told the tragic news, of course, but what if she were to learn it here, in this house, with Byron living just across the street? Mary dared not imagine what

Claire's first wild agony and her fury at Byron might drive her to do. She would surely, and with cause, blame him for her child's death.

The truth must be kept from Claire, Shelley decided, until they could get her away from Pisa. "We must move down to Spezia at once, *at once!* We must be packed and ready to go before the others return so that we can set out without a single moment's delay. We must take any house available. There was one offered us at San Terenzo, near Lerici. It would be possible. Yes, it will have to do. They called it the Casa Magni."

In this mood Shelley was an irresistible torrent. He swept everything before him and refused to listen to any protests. The Williamses arrived with Claire on April 25, and on April 26 Mary, with Claire and little Percy, set off ahead of the others. Trelawny, who had been told of the crisis, escorted them, while Shelley and the Williamses stayed behind to finish the packing. Two cargo vessels had been engaged to transport their household goods down the river to the sea and thence to the little port of Lerici.

Even before the start of the journey Mary was exhausted from the effort of packing, but her pity and concern for Claire somehow sustained her, while Trelawny proved to be an unexpected tower of strength. For all his piratical looks, he was amazingly gentle and understanding. He not only helped Mary to keep their terrible secret but also to soothe Claire's sharp-tongued complaints over what seemed to her such outrageous, unreasonable haste.

Mary's first impression of the Casa Magni was of grimness. The square, fortress-like building stood on the shore at the very edge of the water, set against a dark background of walnut and ilex trees, while beyond loomed a rugged line of mountains. Above an unpaved, open ground floor, a storage space for boats and fishing tackle, ran a long terrace supported by a row of arches. A few outbuildings in the rear housed servants' quarters and a kitchen. No road, only a rough path, connected it with San Terenzo, the primitive fishing village a few hundred yards away.

Slowly, with reluctant foreboding, Mary climbed the steep steps, followed Signor Maglian, their landlord, through the doorway, and looked about her. The bare, whitewashed interior consisted of a single enormous room opening upon the terrace, and four smaller bedrooms. It was dirty, damp, and in disrepair, with cracked ceilings, splotched walls, and broken floors. Mary reacted first with sudden, sharp dismay, then cold horror. Allegra's fate had brought to the surface again her grief for her own lost children and her obsessive fears for little Percy—fears she had struggled long and desperately to fight down. Surely this gloomy, isolated structure, swept by sea winds and salt spray, was no place to bring a delicate child. Such a surge of misery and dread engulfed her that she almost sobbed aloud.

Even Trelawny was for the moment at a loss for words. "It's more like a boathouse than a human habitation," he said, recovering himself. "At least it has a chimney—if only one," he added, in an effort to sound cheerful.

They stayed at an inn in Lerici until May 1, when the

furniture arrived. Shelley and Ned Williams worked all the next day to get the things in place, and on the evening of May 2 they moved in. The Williamses had expected to find another dwelling but there was none to be had, and it was soon clear that the Casa Magni was too small for both families and all their belongings. Somehow most of it was squeezed in under Shelley's insistent direction, but the Williamses and their two children had to be content with one of the four bedrooms. Most of their gear was never unpacked, for Shelley had to have all his books about him.

That day Trelawny left for Genoa, where the two boats were being fitted out, but still no one had told Claire about Allegra. Now, seeing how uncomfortably crowded the house was, she announced that she was returning to Florence. The others quickly gathered in one of the bedrooms and were arguing over how best to break the news when Claire entered unexpectedly, saw the expressions on their faces, and demanded to know the cause. It was Shelley who told her.

Claire's reaction was as wild and terrible as Mary had foreseen. She declared Byron to be the murderer of her child, nor did she spare Mary and Shelley in her passionate grief. *They* had prevented her from kidnapping Allegra out of the horrible convent. *They* were therefore as guilty as Byron. She raged on and on until she finally collapsed and remained barely conscious for several days. Then, with unexpected strength and fortitude, she gathered herself together. "I'm going back to Florence," she said. "I have nothing left to hope for and therefore nothing left to fear."

After Claire's departure, Mary's grief for Allegra submerged her once again in a mood of morbid depression. She could not shake off the sense that disaster brooded over this house, and disaster held only one meaning for her—the loss of little Percy. Shelley too was immensely affected by Allegra's death. One night while walking with Williams along the terrace, he suddenly clutched the other man's arm. "See! There it is!" he cried. When Williams said that he saw nothing, Shelley insisted that he had had a clear vision of Allegra rising out of the moonlit waves and clapping her hands for joy at the sight of him. He could not be quieted until he had rushed inside to Mary and she had taken him into her arms.

But, as before, Shelley was soon able to purge himself of his sorrow by writing verses and by occupying himself with the little flat-bottomed boat. He and Williams took great delight in sailing her around the bay while waiting for their larger vessel to arrive; they were out of doors from morning until night. For this reason the Casa Magni suited them both perfectly, but, to Mary and Jane, housekeeping and the care of the children in such quarters were almost impossibly difficult.

The Tuscan servants they had brought with them disliked the place from the first and several of them left. There were no others to be had at San Terenzo—the people there were a strange, half-savage lot. Moonlit nights brought them out to dance up and down the strand, howling out their wild songs until dawn. By day they had a habit of bathing stark naked on the beach. In this they were often joined happily by Shelley, to Mary's embarrassment and also her terror, for he had still not learned to swim.

For all her placidity, Jane Williams was not always easy to get along with. She was a particular housekeeper; she criticized Mary's lax methods and wished to keep her own saucepans to herself. Mary complained of this to Shelley, who agreed that "it was a pity that anyone so pretty should be so selfish." But he dismissed Mary's brooding fears for Percy's safety. "You are mistaken, Mary," he told her. "This place is far from unhealthy, and the proof of it is that I have not felt better in years. Surely you can see that too? And when our new boat comes it will be perfect."

After a week of cloud and storm in which the wind whistled through the house night and day and the waves beat upon the shore with a sound like cannon fire, the weather cleared. On May 12 in the late afternoon a strange sail rounded the point beyond Spezia and glided into the harbor—their boat had arrived! Trelawny had sent it over from Genoa in the charge of two competent British seamen and a younger sailor boy. To Shelley and Williams, their new toy looked even more beautiful than they had imagined it and, when they tried it out, they found it surprisingly easy to handle.

Trelawny had sent a letter along advising them to keep the crew on for the time being. "It took two tons of iron ballast to bring her down to her bearings and even then she's very crank in a breeze. She's a ticklish craft to handle in rough weather, but with these two good sailors she'll do very well," he explained.

This warning seemed to Williams a slur on his own seamanship. The two older men were therefore dismissed and sent back to Genoa, leaving only the young apprentice seaman, Charles Vivian. A few days later Trelawny came sailing over from Genoa himself on a trial run with Byron's magnificent new schooner, the *Bolivar*. "It would be well to engage a local fisherman who's acquainted with the Gulf," he suggested again to Shelley.

But neither Shelley nor Williams would hear of such a thing. "I can steer her with one hand and hold a copy of Plato in the other," Shelley laughed in answer. "One action is mechanical, the other mental."

After a sail with the two friends in which Shelley's absent-mindedness and inability to follow Williams's orders were painfully obvious, Trelawny drew Williams aside. "You will do no good with Shelley as a crewman until you heave his books and papers overboard, shear the wisps of hair that hang over his eyes, and plunge his arms up to the elbows in a tar bucket!" Trelawny said, but Williams only smiled indulgently.

One thing about the vessel displeased its new owners. Shelley had thought for a while of calling her the *Ariel*, for the sprite in *The Tempest*, but they had finally decided to name her the *Don Juan* as a compliment to Byron's famous poem. Byron had come over to Genoa while the boat was being rigged, and on his orders the name *Don Juan* had been blatantly painted on the white sail in large black letters. This was distasteful to everyone at Casa Magni. "He shan't make a coal barge out of our boat!" Mary protested indignantly. Shelley, Williams, and Vivian therefore scrubbed at the canvas all one day trying to erase the letters, but the result was so blotched and ugly that they had to install a new sail.

For a time Shelley's enthusiasm for his new plaything was so infectious that Mary herself began to share some of his delight, especially when they went sailing over the bay in the evenings, Jane played her guitar, and they all sang together under the summer stars. She would remember these nights forever, Mary thought, and was happy again. At other times, when the sea was calm enough, Shelley took her out in the little landing craft the men had built, the *Lancetta*. Shelley either rowed her about the harbor or, while they floated idly on the waves, read to her from Plato, Calderón, and Keats. Then, if ever, Mary could forget her fears for Percy. The expected baby would be an added comfort, she told herself, for she would no longer have to concentrate all her hopes upon one child.

Then June approached and the weather turned hot—the sort of weather in which Clara and William had each in turn fallen fatally ill—and Mary's spirits plummeted. Her pregnancy was now keeping her wretched most of the time: she became querulous and even snappish, while, through it all, her sense of some dreadful, impending doom weighed mercilessly down upon her.

On June 6 Claire arrived for another visit. Shelley had urged her to come in spite of the crowded condition at Casa Magni. He had written to her that Mary was suffering from "languor and hysterical affections," this at a time when he so greatly needed feminine understanding.

As always, Claire brought discord with her. She lost no time in pointing out to Mary how far she was falling short of her duty to Shelley, whose nature demanded sympathy and warmly demonstrated affection. All this was perhaps true, Mary realized helplessly. But by this time she was really ill and in no state to make any kind of effort. Her condition grew worse and worse until, after days of desperate pain, on June 16 she had a dangerous miscarriage.

She lay for seven hours almost lifeless, for the doctor was late in coming to this remote spot. Jane and Claire struggled devotedly and at the last despairingly to staunch a persistent hemorrhage. It was Shelley who somehow obtained ice and applied it so skillfully that by the time the doctor arrived Mary was out of immediate peril.

Careful nursing restored her somewhat, but she was still exhausted, still utterly drained of the will to live. As she lay slowly getting back her strength in the small, stifling bedroom, the portrait of her mother rose often into her mind, hovering like a loving angel over her. Would she be seeing her at last, and soon? Mary wondered dreamily. How much they would have to say to each other!

More and more often as life began to return, she thought of her little son. Now that her hope of another baby was shattered, she fell once more into the grip of her torturing premonition that she was doomed to lose him as she had lost Clara and William. Why did fate continue to pursue her so cruelly? Could it be that poor Harriet's troubled spirit was somehow demanding atonement from her? The thought was too dreadful to endure. What was more, it implied foolish, irrational superstition, which Godwin's daughter should never entertain, she told herself over and over again.

The others at Casa Magni were now in a highly nervous state also. Shelley had a terrible nightmare and roused the whole household by his screams until, weak as she was, Mary managed to take him into her arms and soothe him as though he were a terrified child. Even calm Jane Williams caught the infection and saw visions of Shelley walking past the terrace windows when he was actually miles away.

On June 19 a letter sent by Leigh Hunt from Genoa announced that they were in Italy at last. Shelley and Williams had planned to sail over to meet and welcome them immediately upon their arrival, but Mary was still far too ill to be left. In the meantime Shelley advised Hunt by letter to sail on and to disembark at Leghorn, for that port would be nearer to the quarters arranged for them at Pisa.

On June 24 Shelley and Williams were aboard the *Don Juan* and about to pull up anchor for Leghorn when Jane Williams came running down to the shore and called them back. Mary had had a relapse and was in a state of hysterical terror at the thought that Shelley was leaving her. They delayed their sailing once again while Shelley tried to quiet Mary's fears with gentle reasoning. "How sad it must be for the Hunts to be stranded in a strange land without the welcoming friends they had expected! And how vitally important it is for me to be there when Hunt meets Byron, to keep him from getting on Byron's nerves at the beginning of their association. Hunt can be tactless, as you know well, Mary. Byron is touchy about his superior rank and is easily offended. The entire success of our long-planned journal depends upon his lordship's support." He also brought a quivering smile to Mary's lips when he referred to Byron, Hunt, and himself as "the eagle, the wren, and the dove" who must somehow become reconciled to sharing the same nest.

Their trip was then set for July 1, and they planned to sail before sunrise in order to reach Leghorn before dark. Mary had promised not to interfere again, but when the day came and she saw them ready to start off in the dawn over the black, restless water, her resolve failed her. She fell to weeping, begged Shelley not to leave her alone in this hateful place, even threatened to take little Percy and go back to the comfort and safety of Pisa. Shelley was gentle and kind, as always, but this time he would not be persuaded to delay the journey. It was only fifty miles to Leghorn, he reminded her. He would be back in a very few days.

At last she consented to let him go, but when he had left

her and boarded the vessel she felt suddenly cold. She went back to her bed and drew the covers up around her, but the chill continued until she was shaking as if with an ague. Weeping and trembling, she lay listening to the slow, inexorable rush and ebb of the waves upon the beach below the house.

CHAPTER FIFTEEN
1822–1823

Morning came at last. Although Mary had not slept, she rose wearily and tried to go about the business of the household. He would be back in a few days, she reminded herself. Surely nothing could happen to little Percy in so short a time. Nevertheless, all day long she hung anxiously over the child or else haunted the terrace, straining her eyes out to sea for a sight of the sail she knew to be well beyond her vision.

A few days later a letter came from Shelley containing much disheartening news. The Hunts had made the extra voyage on to Leghorn safely, but Marianne was clearly in poor health. Shelley had escorted them at once to Pisa and summoned Dr. Vacca to see her. The doctor had pronounced her to be in a "hopeless decline" and of course poor Hunt was terribly upset.

Shelley had installed the Hunt family in the apartment prepared for them on the ground floor of the Casa Lanfranchi. Unfortunately for everyone, Byron had arrived home soon afterward. When he found the six little Hunts playing all over his palace, he had been furious and had promptly stationed his bulldog on the stair landing to keep them out of his quarters. Moreover, he had been inexcusably rude to Marianne Hunt. When Shelley had brought her upstairs to introduce her to his lordship, Byron had barely nodded his head and had not spoken at all.

Now, after Hunt had traveled so far expressly to establish the liberal journal with his help, Byron was making difficulties about that. He had consented to the arrangement, it seemed, only because he had assumed that Leigh Hunt still shared in the ownership of *The Examiner*. Byron had hoped, through Hunt, to gain some influence over that famous publication. Because no one had informed him that Hunt had let it pass out of his hands, Byron now felt that he had been cheated.

Disappointed and vexed, Byron then talked ominously of giving up his house in Pisa, of traveling to America, to Switzerland, to Genoa, or to Lucca. This, of course, would be disastrous for Hunt. Shelley then used every argument he knew and all his powers of persuasion to bring back Byron's interest in the journal which, Shelley was convinced, was so much needed in the world. He had succeeded at last: he had even got Byron's promise to give Hunt the copyright of his satirical poem *The Vision of Judgement* for the first issue. This would, of course, launch their enterprise in fine style, but Shelley was totally exhausted by the long effort. He wished above all things to return to his Mary, but he could not be sure of leaving Leghorn before July 5.

A day or so later Jane received a letter from Ned describing Shelley's troubles in acting as a buffer between Byron and Hunt. Ned added that if Shelley were held up much longer he himself would return in a felucca, one of the small local boats that plied the Gulf. Now it was Jane who took to watching for a sail, joining Mary in her restless vigil.

Monday, July 8, 1822, brought a change of weather—high winds, thunder, and driving gusts of rain. Both women quickly assured each other that their husbands were far too prudent to have set sail in such a storm. Nevertheless, Mary continued to pace the terrace and to stare at the mist-shrouded end of the point of land around which a sail might appear.

Tuesday passed, then Wednesday and Thursday: still no sail and no word. By Friday, Jane had become so alarmed that she tried to get one of the local fishermen to row her over to Lerici for news, but she could find no boatman willing to venture out in so rough a sea. "At least wait until the mail comes—this is the postman's day," Mary begged her.

When the postman arrived he brought a letter, but it came from neither Shelley nor Williams. It was addressed to Shelley, and Mary recognized the handwriting as Leigh Hunt's. She stared at it, feeling her heart begin to pound. "Open it!" Jane and Claire cried almost in the same breath.

Mary's fingers shook so that unfolding the letter was difficult. "Pray write to tell us how you got home, for they say that you had bad weather after you sailed on Monday—" She read Hunt's words aloud that far, then her voice failed.

Jane went ashen. "Then it's all over!" she shrieked, and sank, sobbing, to the floor.

Mary stood motionless, holding the paper in her cold hands. "Hunt is in Pisa," she heard herself whispering. "Not in Leghorn. He could know nothing for certain. Come, we must go to Leghorn and learn the truth."

Desperation gave her a strange new steadiness and strength. She put Claire in charge of the children, bundled Jane into a cloak, and somehow persuaded a reluctant fisherman to row them to Lerici. There Signor Maglian made inquiries for them and reported that no one along the coast had heard so much as a rumor of any disaster. A little cheered, they took a post chaise for Pisa, deciding to go there instead of to Leghorn. If the storm had delayed Shelley, he might have gone back to Pisa to wait it out with Hunt.

They arrived at the Casa Lanfranchi late at night. The sleepy servant who opened the door reported that the Hunts had gone to bed but that his lordship was there and still up. A moment later Teresa Guiccioli appeared at the head of the stairway, surprised by the hour of their visit but smiling in friendly greeting. "Where is Shelley?" Mary gasped out her question in Italian. "Do you know anything of Shelley?" Her face was white as alabaster in the flaring torchlight.

Byron had now joined them. He and the Countess shook

their heads in dismay. "But you are exhausted, you must rest. I'll have a servant prepare beds—" Byron began.

"No," Mary said tonelessly. "We'll go on to Leghorn."

Off they set again through the darkness and arrived at Leghorn at two in the morning. The porter at the inn where they had expected to find Trelawny and Captain Roberts knew nothing of them, and it would be necessary to wait until daylight to ask further. Mary and Jane lay down fully dressed on the beds provided for them, but they did not sleep. At six they were up and out again to ask from inn to inn for the two Englishmen. At the third, the Globe, Captain Roberts came down the stairs to meet them with a look so grave that Jane began to weep again.

Trelawny appeared soon after. He was equally distressed, but he gave them one tenuous strand of hope to cling to. "The *Don Juan* might have been blown by the storm over to Corsica," he said. "It would take several days to receive word from there." In the meantime he urged the two distraught women to return home. He would escort them back himself.

On the way they paused often along the shore for Trelawny to ask at coast-guard stations for news, but he found none until they reached Via Reggio. After making inquiries there, Trelawny walked slowly back to the carriage, his color altered from its healthy bronze. A little boat and a water cask had been picked up by a fishing vessel five miles offshore. The boat was the *Lancetta*, the landing craft in which Mary had floated so happily so short a time before. At her stricken gasp Trelawny continued quickly. "The boat was cumbersome; in bad weather it might have been thrown overboard to lighten the *Don Juan,* as might the water cask too," he told her.

They arrived at San Terenzo at ten o'clock in the evening of July 13 to find it lit by bonfires in celebration of a local fiesta. The villagers were all out singing and dancing along the strand, even in front of the Casa Magni. Trelawny managed to get the attention of one half-drunken fisherman long enough to ask if he had heard any news of Shelley. The man shook his head, grinning, then dashed off into the firelit dark, howling out his wild song against the wind.

There was no rest for anyone that night. Early the next day Trelawny set off on horseback to scour the shore for what he dreaded to find. The coast guard had entered the search too, while Captain Roberts had asked and at once received Lord Byron's permission to use the *Bolivar* for the same purpose. The days that followed in the desolate Casa Magni were, in Mary's words, "a universe of pain, each moment intolerable and giving place to another one still worse."

On Thursday, July 18, Trelawny left for Leghorn in case something might have been heard there. When he had not returned by the evening of the nineteenth, a forlorn hope struggled for life in Mary's mind. "If any"— she choked on the word—"if anything had been found Trelawny would have returned before this to tell . . ."

Her voice died away, for footsteps sounded on the outer stair.

Trelawny appeared in the doorway. At the look on his face Mary and Jane both rose to their feet. "Is there no hope?" Mary whispered.

Trelawny shook his head. He did not speak aloud in answer, but instead turned to the maidservant, Caterina, who had followed him into the room. "Fetch the children, bring them to their mothers," he bade her.

When the shattered women were able to listen, Trelawny told them that on July 15 three bodies had come ashore on three remote and empty stretches of the beach. Italian law was strict in these cases. It ruled that corpses washed ashore must not be removed elsewhere but must be buried at once where they had been found. This had already been done, but, from the detailed official descriptions, Trelawny had identified them definitely as those of Shelley, Williams, and young Vivian.

Trelawny had then appealed to the British minister at Florence. Through his aid, he hoped to be granted permission to disinter them and hold ceremonies of cremation there on the sands beside the sea. It seemed to Trelawny that this was something Shelley would have wished. It was the ancient Greek custom, he reminded the agonized young widows, and was not Shelley himself an ancient Greek in spirit? The ashes could then be taken away to wherever they wished them buried.

After this, as Mary wrote later, instead of offering

futile sympathy, Trelawny "launched forth into overflowing and eloquent praise of Shelley." It was so sincere, so spontaneous, and so heartfelt that it served somehow to ease a little of Mary's pain. She spoke of it often afterward, profoundly grateful to this rough man of action for his instinctive knowledge of what could help her through those first searing hours.

The next morning it was Trelawny who took the bereft women and children away from haunted, sea-echoing Casa Magni back to their old quarters at Pisa in the Tre Palazzi, where they would be among their friends. It was Trelawny, during the weeks that followed, who attended to an endless series of grim details. He interviewed officials, wrote out petitions in due form, signed papers, and paid fees until permission was at last granted for the funeral ceremonies he had planned.

It was he again who hired workmen and supervised them while the bodies were disinterred and cremated, Williams on August 15, Shelley on the sixteenth, for they had come ashore far apart and could not be moved from those locations. It was Trelawny who built the funeral pyres with his own hands, each in turn, on those two stretches of golden sand between the mountains and the sea. It was he who watched over the harrowing conflagrations through long hours until the end, while the *Bolivar* waited offshore; he who poured wine, salt, honey, and incense, in the ancient Greek fashion, over the pitiful remains of his friends. Greatly moved, Trelawny noted that one solitary sea bird circled all day long high above

Shelley's burning pyre, its wings flashing white as it turned endlessly against the blue Italian sky.

Along with a horde of officials and curious onlookers, Byron and Hunt attended the ceremonies also, but they reported themselves far too crushed to give any aid. It was Trelawny, therefore, who gathered up the ashes after they had cooled and placed them in the small wooden chests he had had made for that purpose. Ned Williams's ashes were to be returned to England, but, at Mary's request, Trelawny sent Shelley's to Rome in care of the English consul, there to be buried in the English cemetery beside those of his son, William, and not far from the grave of Keats.

"We saw sorrow in other faces," Mary wrote to Trelawny later, "but we found help only from you."

Trelawny even offered to provide Mary with money to return at once to England if she wished. She refused him gently and with tears in her eyes for his unselfish kindness, for she knew from many signs that he was half in love with her and also that he had very little money to spare. She was still unable to think clearly enough to make any firm decision about her future. Meanwhile, she would stay on in Italy with the Hunts.

Settled once again in Pisa, Mary moved through the days like an automaton, her heart leaden within her. Adding to the bitterness of her grief was the knowledge that during these last months she had allowed her own illness and her fears for little Percy once again to build a barrier between herself and Shelley. She had failed her beloved at the last, and she could now sense that Shelley's friends felt that too.

Hunt was hinting at it more and more often lately—that Mary had been cold and unsympathetic, unworthy of Shelley's love, and therefore had forfeited it. There was now no one, no one at all in whom she could confide, nowhere to turn except to her journal. Into it, from that time on, she poured out her adoration, her remorse, her longings, and her dream of someday being reunited with "mine own Shelley." Losing him had erased all his imperfections from her mind. He was now a celestial being, one whom the blind world had misjudged. She therefore solemnly dedicated the rest of her life not only to caring for Shelley's son but also to helping mankind to appreciate Shelley's divine goodness and matchless genius.

During this time there seemed to be countless routine things that had to be done and Mary was the only one who could do most of them. Much as she loathed Casa Magni, she had to return there to watch over the packing and shipping of their possessions back to Pisa, most notably Shelley's many books and papers. Shelley had named Peacock and Lord Byron as executors of his will: Mary had to write at once to give Peacock the news and to ask him for funds. She had spent much of what she had to send Claire on her way to join her brother Charles in Vienna and to help Jane and her children return to her family in England. There was very little left for herself.

She did not worry about this in the beginning, for Byron

had said that she could call upon him for whatever she needed. He was all kindness at first; he and the Countess visited Mary almost every day. As an executor, he took it upon himself to open negotiations with Shelley's father in Mary's behalf. In reply Sir Timothy stated bluntly and at once that he considered Mary one of the chief causes of his son's deplorable conduct and would do exactly nothing for her or her child. Shelley's son Charles by his first marriage was now his heir and he refused to acknowledge any claim made for little Percy.

Mary saw Jane off in September; they both shed many tears as they said goodbye. With Jane, Mary sent a letter of introduction to Shelley's friend Hogg, hoping that he might call upon her and so learn more of Shelley's last days. Soon after this Byron decided to move from Pisa to a villa near Genoa, for the Pisan authorities were making things difficult for Teresa's father and brother and therefore distressing her. It was necessary, of course, for the Hunts to go too, and Mary went along with them. With Jane and Claire gone and Trelawny often absent, she clung to these friends and looked forward to sharing the rooms she had engaged for them in the Casa Negroto.

Byron had made no secret of the fact that this time he did not want the Hunts in his villa. "Mrs. Hunt's children are dirtier and more mischievous than Yahoos—was there ever such a kraal out of the Hottentot country?" he said in a complaining note to Mary.

This criticism of her adored Marianne greatly upset

Mary at the time, but before long she felt almost inclined to agree with his lordship. Even by Mary's easy standards Marianne was an impossible housekeeper and her children were entirely undisciplined. They teased poor Percy so unmercifully that Mary never dared to leave him alone with any of them. The result was that the only time she had for the writing with which she hoped to raise some money, or for the task of sorting over Shelley's papers and manuscripts, was at night when Percy was safe in bed. It was out of the question to try to work in the living rooms, where the older Hunts talked incessantly and the children played their noisy games. Her own small room became her only refuge; then, when cold weather set in, her stove smoked so much that after a few attempts she dared not light it.

Mary had not written news of Shelley's death to her father. He had learned of it by chance and now he wrote to reproach her for her neglect. He expressed no real sorrow for her loss except to suggest that since she now shared his own state of misfortune they should draw together to console each other. He had been declared bankrupt and had had to give up the Skinner Street house, he told her. He assumed that she would soon be returning to England. In that case, his own quarters in the Strand, meager though they were, would be hers to share until she could find a place of her own.

Return to England? The question loomed larger and more menacing as she shivered in her tiny room. Her mind as well as her hands seemed numbed with the cold. She could not decide. Her father in later letters urged her to come, stating that *Frankenstein* had been so successful that there was every reason to believe that she could earn a living by her writing *if* she were there in London. Peacock too felt that the chance of Sir Timothy's changing his mind about Percy would be far better if the boy were near at hand. Mary did not care how the baronet felt about herself, but, of course, small Percy's future had to be considered.

Oh, but her heart was here in Italy! How could she go so far from the places where Shelley had chosen to live and where he now lay? Then there were the Hunts. Friction between Byron and Leigh Hunt had been growing ever since Shelley's death. Mary felt that she could help the Hunts by championing them as Shelley had done, but in this she was sadly mistaken. Her efforts not only were futile but were irritating to Byron: he was beginning to dislike her along with the whole Hunt family. Of the many generous promises of aid he had made to Mary, no cash had been forthcoming except thirty-six pounds in payment for an article she had written for *The Liberal*, as they now called their journal. Byron's sense of obligation, struggling vainly with his parsimony, made him angry and resentful whenever he met the clear gaze of Mary's eyes.

Moreover, Byron was growing restless. He was tiring of Teresa Guiccioli and the problems of her relatives, the Gambas. He deeply regretted his involvement with Hunt and *The Liberal*. The first number of the journal had appeared in London on October 15, and it had met with much criticism. Byron's friends in England were advising him to disassociate himself from the project, which, they wrote, was injuring his own reputation. He began to talk of going to Greece to join in the fight for liberation, but neither Mary nor Trelawny believed that these plans would ever materialize. Byron was far too indolent and pleasure-loving to engage in any such harsh adventure, they told each other.

Early in January of 1823 Sir Timothy's lawyer, Whitton, wrote to Byron to say that if Mary would give little Percy into his grandfather's charge he would make her a small yearly pension. Give up her child? Mary would far sooner give up her life! She refused the offer at once, but after that her problem loomed larger than ever. The funds which had come to Shelley from his grandfather's estate were now cut off from her. If her writing was to be her only resource, she must return to England—yet how was she to get there? The journey would require money and she was all but penniless.

She struggled with the question all during the spring. Trelawny had gone off on a hunting trip into the Maremma marshes, and Mary missed his sympathetic company. Even his brusque criticism of what he called her "mood of self-absorbed misery." From the Maremma he had gone to Rome, and he wrote to Mary from there that he had been arranging the planting of "six young cypresses and four laurels" in front of the recess where Shelley's ashes were buried. On Shelley's stone he had had engraved lines from *The Tempest*, Shelley's favorite of all of Shakespeare's plays.

> Nothing of him that doth fade
> But doth suffer a sea-change
> Into something rich and strange.

Lately, Trelawny wrote, Byron had been asking him to go along with him to Greece, and the Cornishman, convinced at last that his lordship was really in earnest, was half inclined to accept. It was the sort of project he liked; he knew and loved Greece well. Byron had chartered a ship and was fitting it out handsomely—he could spend money to gratify his own wishes, it seemed.

In mid-June, Trelawny rode up from Rome into Genoa on a fine Hungarian cavalry horse he had lately purchased, ready to join the Greek expedition. He found much to criticize in the ship, the brig *Hercules*, but he approved the arms and ammunition Byron was having loaded aboard her. As for the elaborate scarlet and gold uniforms and the huge plumed helmets Byron had had made expressly for himself, Trelawny, and Pietro Gamba, Trelawny guffawed at them and refused to try his on, to the great disappointment of Byron.

So Lord Byron was really going off to fight for the glory that was Greece! Mary had not believed that it would ever happen, but the possibility now moved her to ask him for the last time for the money he had promised months before to finance her journey back to England. Unfortunately she made the request through Hunt. He put the question tactlessly, even referring to the thousand-pound wager Byron had lost to Shelley as a debt of honor which should of course be paid to Mary. At this Byron flew into a rage and refused with utter and cruel finality. Learning of this, Trelawny made his own generous offer again, made it so eloquently in the name of his love for Shelley that Mary could not refuse.

On July 17 the *Hercules,* with Byron and Trelawny aboard, sailed for Greece, and a week later Mary Shelley and her two-year-old son started back to England to face whatever lay in store for them there.

CHAPTER SIXTEEN
1823 – 1828

During her last weeks in Italy, Mary had managed to smooth out her differences with the Hunts and they parted the best of friends. Mary wrote a cheerful letter back to them describing an especially lovely spot on her homeward journey and saying that someday they might all live together again here. Each member of both families would do some task; all would work in harmony.

"Marianne shall make puddings and pies, to make up for the vegetables and meat I shall boil and spoil. Thorny shall sweep the room, Mary make the beds, Johnny clean the kettles and pans and then we will pop him into the many streams hereabouts and so clean him. Swinny, being so quick, shall be our Mercury, Percy Hunt our gardener, Sylvan and Percy Florence our weeders and Vincent our plaything."

Traveling, with no one to help her care for her lively two-year-old, was tiring, and Mary paused in Paris for a much-needed rest with some good friends, the John Kenneys. There she visited the Horace Smiths too, and at the home of another acquaintance met a young American actor-dramatist named John Howard Payne. Payne's acting and playwriting were undistinguished, but he is nevertheless well remembered as the writer of the song *Home, Sweet Home.*

The Channel crossing was blessedly calm for once. On August 25, 1823, a few days before her twenty-sixth birthday, Mary and little Percy were met at the wharf and escorted up to London by her father and her half brother William. She was deeply touched to be received so kindly by her still-beloved father, but *London!* Dull, leaden-gray, interminable streets under dull gray skies, people with pinched and sober faces hurrying past on errands that were surely as dull and gray as themselves! After Italy's sunshine and vivid color Mary's heart sank as though it were fashioned out of heavy, dull, gray lead.

The Godwins' house in the Strand proved to be far too small to contain such conflicting personalities as Mrs. Godwin and Mary. Mamma's welcome to the prodigals was an all-too-obvious effort. She was kind to Percy Florence, but it was soon clear that she blamed Mary for every misfortune that had happened to Claire. Worst of all, she gave Mary to understand that Shelley and all he stood for were best not mentioned in her presence. For the time being, however, there was no place else for Mary and her child to go.

Much of William Godwin's cordial welcome to his daughter, she soon learned, derived from the fact that at that very moment a dramatization of her novel *Franken-*

stein was running successfully in London. Her father and William took Mary to see it a few days after her arrival. "Lo and behold, I found myself famous!" Mary wrote to the Hunts. She herself could not really believe in or quite enjoy the play's acclaim; she actually resented the praise showered upon her when Shelley's name seemed to be now so utterly forgotten in England. Her divine Shelley, whose work was to hers as the sun to a tallow candle!

Mary received no payment from either her novel *Valperga* or from the play, however. She had signed her royalties from the book over to Godwin in return for his placing it with a publisher and there had been no arrangements about dramatic rights for *Frankenstein*. In desperate need of funds, she summoned up the courage to call on Sir Timothy's lawyer, Mr. Whitton. After a series of futile and humiliating interviews, Whitton at last gave Mary an advance of one hundred pounds and the assurance that Sir Timothy would probably allow her the same sum every year for his grandson's care. This was on the stern condition, however, that if she should publish a biography of Shelley during the baronet's lifetime, the allowance would be forfeited.

In this now-alien land, in this house where Shelley's name, if spoken at all, brought only disapproving silence, loneliness closed in around Mary, terrible, bleak loneliness. She ached for contact with someone, anyone, who had known and loved Shelley. Trelawny, her stalwart mainstay, was now far away, fighting in Greece, and no word had come from him for a long time. Even Claire's letters were welcome now, but they were few and far between and always full of bitter complaints over her hard lot as the governess of disagreeable brats.

Jane Williams was living in London in the district known as Kentish Town. Mary had hastened to call upon her when she first arrived in England, but she was disturbed and baffled by a subtle change in her friend. Mary had supposed that Jane would be as eager as she was for them to establish and share a home for their three orphaned children; they had planned such an arrangement during Jane's final weeks in Italy. Did they not already share the dearest as well as the most tragic memories?

To Mary's surprise and disappointment, Jane seemed entirely satisfied with her present manner of living and reluctant to make any change. Mary therefore stayed on with the Godwins, working to the point of exhaustion on the collecting of Shelley's all-but-forgotten manuscripts into what was to be a volume of posthumous poems. This would be the first step in the task to which she had dedicated every atom of her powers—the exalting of Shelley's name and his genius before the world. Leigh Hunt's brother John had promised to publish the book, but only after three of Shelley's admirers—Bryan Procter, Thomas Lovell Beddoes, and Thomas Forbes Kelsall—had been induced by Mary to assume the monetary risk.

By the spring of 1824 Mary had found that she could earn enough money by writing articles for journals to move into rooms of her own. She chose Kentish Town in order to be near Jane Williams, who still represented her most precious bond with the past. Mary's devotion to Jane was complete. Was she not the one being on earth who had shared and endured her loss? Jane tried to be kind, but she was basically a vain and shallow woman. She had already put her grief for Ned far behind her and was vastly enjoying the attentions of someone else. Mary's continual harping on their mutual tragedy embarrassed and bored her. She had even begun an effort to shake off Mary's too-clinging friendship, until she discovered that Mary—now, because of *Frankenstein*, a literary celebrity—was being invited to many interesting gatherings.

In Italy, Mary had always enjoyed parties and social evenings far more than Shelley had. After attending a few of these in London, however, she had decided to decline any more such invitations. How could she bear to go where her own work was praised while Shelley's name brought only polite little murmurs of sympathy for her but no appreciation of his genius? It was Jane Williams who finally persuaded her to accept a few invitations by promising to go with her.

They therefore visited the Gisbornes together and had evening tea in the home of Mary's old friends Charles and Mary Lamb. There Mary renewed her acquaintance with the Vincent Novellos, whose sixteen-year-old daughter, also named Mary, wrote a description of Mary Shelley as she saw her then:

"Her well-shaped, golden-haired head, almost always a little bent; her marble-white shoulders and arms, statuesquely visible in the perfectly plain black velvet dress which the custom of that time allowed to be cut low . . . her thoughtful, earnest eyes; her short upper lip and intellectually curved mouth . . . her exquisitely-formed white, dimpled hands, with rosy palms and fingers tapered into tips as slender as a Vandyke portrait."

At some of Godwin's evenings Mary saw many other old friends—Hazlitt, of course, and Coleridge, whose reading of *The Ancient Mariner* had so moved her as a child. Her new acquaintances included the American authors Washington Irving and James Fenimore Cooper, who had served as Godwin's American agent. But in Godwin's house mention of Shelley still was met either by stony silence or, at best, by vague and evasive words—words spoken kindly out of consideration for his lovely, fragile-looking young widow. After one such encounter Mary turned to her journal, addressing herself to Shelley as she now so often did. "I have been gay in company tonight," she confessed to him. "And yet, my own, never was I so entirely yours . . . I cling to your memory alone and you alone receive the overflowing of my heart. Beloved Shelley, good night."

The volume of Shelley's *Posthumous Poems* was published early in 1824. It received several favorable reviews and Mary's hope soared high. Now, surely, the blind world would begin to appreciate the treasure it had rejected so cruelly! Three hundred copies had been sold when Sir Timothy learned that his erring son's name had appeared again in the public press. Furious, he sent word to Mary through Whitton that all unsold copies must be withdrawn and, if any other work of his son's should appear, Mary's allowance for Percy would be abruptly stopped.

This was a bitter and shattering blow. For a time Mary was rebellious and ready to defy the old gentleman, but the thought of her boy's future overruled her own desires. Sir Timothy was, after all, over seventy; he could not live much longer and after he was gone she could publish anything she pleased. She consented to the recall of the unsold books, then turned with renewed determination to her own heavy schedule of writing. She worked not only on articles and translations but also on a novel she had already begun. It was to have, as its finest character, a man who would portray her beloved but, of course, under another name.

On May 14 a rumor swept through London, then blazed like wildfire all over England. *Byron is dead!* He had died at Missolonghi, in Greece, where he had gone to fight for Liberty.

Mary was shocked, saddened, and also deeply stricken with remorse. How could she have so doubted Byron's sincerity of purpose? Generously she now erased all his faults and unkindnesses from her memory and tried to recall only the gay, handsome, charming Albé of their Geneva days, the Albé who had admired and appreciated her Shelley and who had been so kind to her during the first weeks of her loss.

Once again she heard his unforgettable voice and Shelley's answering it in their night-long conversations, heard his Tyrolean song blown back across the windy lake. "Beauty sat upon his countenance and power beamed from his eye," she wrote of Byron in her journal.

Two months later Byron's funeral procession moved slowly and solemnly through the silent, crowded streets of London. Mary watched it from her windows and thought with tearful sympathy of poor Teresa, now as bereft as she herself had been almost exactly two years before. The cortege had hardly passed when Mary received a letter from Thomas Medwin stating that he was now preparing a book—*Memoirs of Lord Byron*—based on notes taken during conversations in Pisa. He asked Mary's help with it, for he planned to make Shelley "a very prominent being in the work."

Mary had never liked Medwin; she distrusted both his ability and his motives. She felt that it was almost indecent of him to plan to "grow fat upon the world's love of tittle-tattle," as she wrote to Marianne Hunt. Besides, there was the ban Sir Timothy had placed upon any biography of Shelley written by her. Medwin might think her name an asset and use it, and that would of course anger Sir Timothy. She therefore refused her aid. Some time later he wrote again, offering to suppress the publication if she would pay him a sum of money in return, a form of blackmail which Mary courageously defied. When Medwin's book appeared, it was found to be so clumsily written that it received little notice.

Study, writing, and the care of her sturdy, happy little son now crowded Mary's hours. In the evenings there were sometimes parties and then, at night, there was always her journal into which she could pour out her emotions. She continued to see Jane Williams almost daily and soon learned that Jane was being courted by none other than Thomas Jefferson Hogg! The letter of introduction which Mary had sent to him with Jane had brought them together, and their friendship, thus begun, had warmed to love.

Hogg, it seemed, not only was Shelley's friend and disciple; he was also highly susceptible to any woman who had ever won Shelley's interest and affection—first Harriet, then Mary herself, and now Jane! Mary was delighted at the prospect of a match between the two and urged Jane to marry him, even though this left Mary more alone than ever.

She herself had admirers, even suitors. Among them was the young American whom she had first met in Paris, John Howard Payne. He was presently having some success on the London stage and he had fallen head over heels in love with the romantically beautiful young widow whose past was so filled with tragedy. He showered letters upon her; she answered them graciously and accepted the theater tickets he sent her, for she had always loved the stage. She made it clear, however, that Shelley was the one and only love of her life. She could not possibly marry anyone unless he could equal Shelley's stature as man and genius —an impossible standard, as they both knew.

Mary's novel *The Last Man* was published in 1826. It pictured a world in which a pestilence raged through every continent and finally swept away all of mankind but one—the writer of the book. It brought some praise from the critics and public and is still read, but it provided only meager financial returns. A prominent character, Adrian, was clearly a portrait of Shelley seen through Mary's adoring eyes, and Hogg recognized the likeness. "The character of Adrian is most happy and just," he wrote Mary. Another of the characters, Lord Raymond, depicted Byron so vividly that Claire wrote a bitter letter of protest; her hatred of Byron had grown with the years.

In that same autumn of 1826, the death of Charles, Shelley's young son by his first marriage, forced Sir Timothy against his will to change his attitude toward small Percy. Mary's boy was now the direct heir to the baronetcy, a person of importance whose place in the family must now be acknowledged. Sir Timothy still refused to see Mary, but he made a slightly more ample, if grudging, allowance for her son.

During the next two years fate seemed at last to be dealing more gently with Mary. She was now a well-established writer and would have had an almost adequate income from her hard, incessant work if Godwin had not continued to demand and to receive help from her. Little Percy's education and his future now seemed assured. Shelley's will had been adjudged valid: someday, after Sir Timothy's death, Mary herself would be well off. The will had made generous provision for Claire, for the Hunts, and even for Hogg.

Mary had by now achieved a respected place among the

most interesting people in London and, after her stormy years with Shelley as a scorned outcast from English society, she was finding the sensation genuinely pleasant. Among her new friends was the Irish poet Tom Moore, who had been a close friend of Byron's. Mary liked him as soon as they met, enjoyed his genial company, and respected his talent. When he asked for her help in writing a *Life of Lord Byron*, she consented gladly. She even wrote to Teresa Guiccioli and secured from her an account of Byron's life with her in Italy.

But the one overriding purpose in Mary's life was still the advancement before the world of Shelley's fame as philosopher and poet, and this was still blocked by Sir Timothy's harsh decree. She nevertheless continued to plan for the future publication of all his verses. She planned, too, to write his biography—a formidable and harrowing task for her, as she knew well, one which would need far more strength and courage than she now possessed. All this would have to wait until the old baronet's demise, which, she continued to assure herself, could not be far away. Like the impatient Claire, she had now begun to refer to her father-in-law as "Old Time."

Mary visited Jane and Hogg frequently, still finding her dearest refuge and solace in the memories they all shared of her lost love. Life seemed to be going reasonably well for her until, in the fall of 1828, her merciless schedule of work wore down her strength so much that she fell ill. During this time of weakness she sank into one of her moods of depression. It brought, as before, a haunting presentiment that some new danger was looming upon her horizon. She wrote of it in her journal. "How very dark the future seems—I shrink in fear from the mere imagination of coming time. Is any evil about to approach me? Have I not suffered enough?"

As always, her fears centered quickly upon little Percy, although the boy, now nine years old, seemed exceptionally strong and healthy. Then the blow fell. It came from such an unexpected quarter that Mary was defenseless against it.

For some time past, Mary learned, Jane had been entertaining Hogg and his friends by telling spitefully amusing tales of her life in Italy with the Shelleys. She described Shelley to her delighted listeners as a grotesque, ludicrous creature, outlandish in his clothes and his habits, who had fallen madly in love with her. Not only had he given her many expensive presents but he had written the most ridiculously exaggerated love poems and songs to her. Jane had been kind to him merely out of pity, she explained, because his wife, Mary, was making his life so miserable with her jealousy and her bad-tempered whining.

The wound cut so deep that for a time Mary was numbed into helplessness. She knew that she must refute these vicious lies, but how? Longing for Trelawny's steadfast presence and advice, she remembered, too late, that although he had been tremendously fond of Ned, he had neither liked nor trusted Jane. At last Mary turned to Tom Moore for counsel. He confessed that some of those stories had reached his ears also, and he persuaded Mary to write directly to Jane and to demand that she not only stop her cruel gossip but contradict it at once.

When they next met, Jane, who wept easily, burst into a dramatic flood of tears and begged Mary's forgiveness. "I never meant to hurt *you!*" she sobbed. "It was just idle chatter, just an effort to be amusing, just foolish exaggeration for effect. If you had not hung over me so constantly with unwanted advice, as though I were some ignorant younger sister, I would never have done it."

Honest, loyal Mary tried her best to understand and to pardon the woman whom she had believed to be her best friend, but the hurt remained. Her journal records the bitter sense that Jane had marred the past for her and left an indelible stain upon it, had taken much of the sweetness from the memories to which she clung so desperately.

CHAPTER SEVENTEEN
1828–1851

Mary endured Jane Williams's cruel betrayal of their friendship somehow, as she had so much else in her troubled life. By midsummer she had rallied enough to accept an invitation to give some lectures in Paris. While there she contracted smallpox—a light case but enough to mar her fair complexion for a time and temporarily dull the bright sheen of her hair. On her return to England, a few weeks at a seaside resort effected a complete cure and she was left without a scar—a solace to her womanly vanity which she much needed.

Cordial letters had been coming from Trelawny lately at irregular intervals and that same fall he reappeared in England. Mary then met him for the first time since he had sailed off with Byron on their ill-fated Greek adventure. She was delighted to see him; she could never forget his kindness and generosity to her when she had needed it most, but she found him sadly changed. He was gaunt, wasted, and irritable, still suffering from a lingering fever contracted during the campaign.

He soon found England intolerable, and early in Feb-

ruary 1829, he returned to Florence. From there his letters
to Mary became more affectionate than ever, even ardent.
In one he suggested that Fate, without their choice, might
soon unite them. "And who can control his fate?" he asked.

Mary was truly fond of him over and above her gratitude. But marriage? He had courted Claire unsuccessfully
for a while, she knew; in his letters he often boasted of
conquests among Greek and Italian girls and of at least
one illegitimate child. While in Greece he had married the
sister of Odysseus, one of the Greek leaders, although that
marriage had been later dissolved.

Mary's answer was as tactful as she could make it. "I am
not so young as I was when you first knew me, but I am
as proud," she wrote. "I must have the entire devotion of
anyone who will win me. You belong to womankind in
general. . . . Mary Shelley shall be written on my tomb.
It is so pretty a name that I never should have the heart
to get rid of it."

Trelawny now announced that he was making plans to
write the story of his adventurous career, and it was to contain much about Byron and Shelley as he knew them. Like
Medwin, he asked Mary to supply him with material con-
cerning Shelley's life and, as she had with Medwin, she
refused. At that time she had no faith in Trelawny's writing ability, and she knew also his talent for exaggeration—
even outright fabrication—to make a good story. What was
perhaps most important, she still hoped to write Shelley's
biography herself someday when Sir Timothy would no
longer be an obstacle.

This rebuff angered Trelawny, who was already nettled by Mary's rejection of his hinted offer of marriage, and he never quite forgave the two injuries she had done to his vanity. He continued the work, and when he finished it he sent the manuscript on to Mary, nevertheless, for her criticism and also for her help in finding him a publisher. On reading it Mary acknowledged generously that she had misjudged his writing skill. She also suggested some alterations to conform with the changing taste of the times. After disputing these hotly, Trelawny finally agreed to them, and Mary arranged for the book's publication. It appeared under the title *The Adventures of a Younger Son.*

By this time, due to unremitting and exhausting work on articles and translations as well as novels, Mary was making enough money to enable her to move to a better address in London. She could now entertain modestly in her own quarters; her small parties became very popular with the literary set. People who met her for the first time often expressed surprise at her manner and appearance. From the vigor of her writing they had expected a formidable "bluestocking" type of woman, whereas she was small, slim, delicately made, quiet, entirely feminine, and even shy.

The opera, plays, races at Ascot, a party at the Speaker's were among the festive outings Mary began to enjoy at this time. In 1830 she even attended the coronation of King William IV, "on the second bench in the Earl Marshall's box—the best in the Abbey," she noted in her diary. "They were so stingy the poor King was obliged to poke with his pen and the Duke of Devonshire to tilt the inkstand—to get out enough to write his name" was her added wry comment.

In 1832 Sir Timothy's lawyer, Whitton, died and was succeeded by a man named Gregson. Gregson proved to be far more sympathetic to Mary and her needs than Whitton had been, and through him she was able at last to get permission to publish a comprehensive edition of Shelley's poetry—but still no biography.

Preparing and editing this took years of exacting work, for Mary had decided to add notes to almost every poem, notes in which she could tell where and how Shelley had come to write each one and what it had meant to him. These notes—invaluable insights into the poet's life and philosophy—still managed not to run counter to Sir Timothy's ban on an actual biography.

That same year, 1832, marked a milestone in young Percy's life. Mary remembered that Shelley had expressed the wish for his son to attend one of England's great public schools, but when she suggested Eton, where Shelley had been, Sir Timothy utterly forbade it. Mary then chose Harrow, Lord Byron's school, much to Claire's indignation.

Percy's first term at Harrow passed very happily, but Mary soon discovered that her income would not cover his expenses as a boarding pupil. Therefore, the following spring, she gave up her London home and moved into lodgings in the small, quiet village of Harrow so that Percy could still attend the school as a day scholar. This change meant that Mary was now cut off from the pleasant London circle she had begun to enjoy so much, but when it was a question of Percy's education she could not choose otherwise. Her letters and her journal at that time describe the dull and desolate loneliness of her life during those years, brightened only by Percy's companionship and that of the many young friends he brought home to meet her, for the boy was greatly liked by his classmates.

In 1833, largely through Mary's efforts, Godwin was granted a position as Yeoman Usher of the Exchequer, a place which carried with it a small pension and also living quarters. Now, for the first time in many years, he no longer strained his daughter's slender resources. What was more, Mary's next novel, *Lodore,* proved to be a financial success. Like *The Last Man,* it contained much autobiographical material. The character of Lodore himself was based on that of Lord Byron, whose imperious presence still filled Mary's mind far more than she realized or, if she did, would admit. This, of course, brought more angry and sarcastic comments from Claire.

Trelawny was back in England. His autobiography had been published, and the adventurous tale, combined with his picturesque personality, vastly intrigued the public. He was now much sought after by fine ladies of fashion for their parties. For all his lingering resentment toward Mary for her refusal of him, he kept in touch with her, partly to scold her for what he called her "namby-pamby primness," partly to describe his triumphs to her, and often to ask her for favors. One of these was to take his young illegitimate daughter into her home for a three-month visit. Writing to Claire at the same time, he described Mary as growing "hopelessly conservative."

Others, particularly feminists of her day, had expressed surprise and disappointment that Mary, the wife of Shelley and the daughter of Godwin and Mary Wollstonecraft, was not more deeply involved in the liberal movement which had finally managed in June of 1832 to pass the great and historic Reform Bill. In her journal Mary gave her own private answers to these critics. "My parents and Shelley had a passion for reforming the world. As for myself, I earnestly desire the good and enlightenment of my fellow-creatures and see all, in the present course, tending to the same and rejoice; but I am not for violent extremes which only bring on injurious reaction." How well she had learned that!

"I have never said a word in disfavor of liberalism; that I have not supported it openly in writing arises from the following causes, as far as I know: (1) That I have not argumentative powers: I see things pretty clearly but I cannot demonstrate them. (2) I recoil from the vulgar abuse of the inimical press—I act on the defensive, an inglorious position. (3) My horror of pushing and inability to put myself forward unless cherished and supported. [Her shyness was still a handicap, it seems.] (4) Radicals repel me—they are violent without sense of justice—selfish, rude, envious and insolent—talking without knowledge."

In this same vein, when a friend suggested that she make more of an effort to teach young Percy to think for himself, Mary burst out with the unconsciously self-revealing reply —"My God! Let him learn to think like other people!" It seemed that Trelawny was right. Mary Wollstonecraft's daughter had come around full circle in her thinking: forced there by the harsh discipline of her life.

A year later another entry in Mary's diary showed that she was still haunted by a sense of guilt over the tragedy of Shelley's first wife. This she had never confessed to anyone, for would not such an admission be disloyal to Shelley? In her journal she referred to "poor Harriet, to whose sad fate I attribute so many of my own heavy sorrows, as the atonement claimed by fate for her death."

In 1835 William Godwin died, and Mary arranged, with the help of an influential friend, Mrs. Caroline Norton, to get his pension continued for her stepmother and so provided for Mamma's comfort for the remainder of her life. The next year Percy went up to Cambridge and entered Trinity College. At last Mary was able to move back to the social life of London. If fate had indeed demanded an atonement from her, it seemed that by this time it must have been paid in full. With the beginning of the reign of Victoria, the new young queen, in 1837, life began actually to smile upon Mary Shelley.

First and supremely important, in 1838 she was able to publish her complete collection of Shelley's poems. The long effort of preparing and editing them had drained her fragile strength to exhaustion, but her heart told her that she had done her task well. She had vowed somehow to portray Shelley before the hostile and doubting world as she knew him to be—a radiant, loving, noble genius—and through the medium of the notes she had attached to his poems she felt that she had succeeded. The volume received a good deal of attention and many favorable as well as unfavorable notices. But at least his work was there for all to read, and, once read, it could never be forgotten—a monument mightier and more lasting than any built of marble. Mary was serenely sure of that.

In 1840, when Percy Florence came of age, his grandfather raised his allowance to four hundred pounds a year. To Mary's happy astonishment one of the first things her son did was to invite her to accompany him and some of his friends on a trip to the Continent during their summer holidays. Mary hesitated to accept: surely they didn't really want her along! At her age—she was forty-two—and in her poor state of health, might she not be a burden on their plans? Percy insisted, however, and also arranged for a maid to accompany her.

In spite of the poignant memories that it evoked, the journey through the Rhine country and into Italy was pleasant for Mary until they reached Lake Como in Italy. There Percy took it into his head to have a sailboat built to use on the lake, a boat he designed himself especially for speed! Tortured by the recollection of his father's fate, Mary paced the shore, cold with dread, all the time he and his friends were on the water, and she was relieved beyond words when they finally left Como for Milan.

When the holiday time ended, the students had to return to their classes, but Mary stayed on in Milan for a while longer and from there traveled to Geneva. After a nostalgic glimpse of their beloved little Maison Chapuis and Byron's Villa Deodati, she returned home by way of Paris, where she stopped for a brief visit with Claire. Notes she made during these weeks appeared later in the form of a book entitled *Rambles in Germany and Italy*.

Other, longer stays on the Continent followed and then, in 1844, the unbelievable happened. Sir Timothy died at last at the age of ninety-two. Percy Florence succeeded to the baronetcy and the estate and, with his mother, moved into Field Place, where Shelley had spent his lively, happy boyhood. Unfortunately the great house soon proved to be difficult to run with the staff they could afford, for by this time the family fortune had been greatly depleted by Sir Timothy's determination to give away as much of it as was legally possible to his younger son, John Shelley. Then, too, there were the ruinous post-obits which Shelley had signed so rashly long ago and which must be paid from his son's inheritance.

Now, after twenty-two years, Mary was free to write the biography of Shelley which she had put off for so long. She started in upon it eagerly and bravely, but the emotional effort soon proved too much for her. Her health failed and, after a struggle, she was forced to give up the task. Shelley's published poems were receiving more and more attention and even, in some quarters, acclaim, although never as much as Mary felt they deserved. Someone else would have to take up the writing of his life, she told herself. It would not be their son, as she had once hoped. Percy was sunny-hearted, charming, and affectionate, but his interests were not in the least literary.

Now, too, the bequests Shelley had made in his will could be paid at last. He had provided generously for Claire, for Hunt, and also for Hogg, and Mary carried out his wishes with scrupulous care. Many legal complications were involved, and those delays brought much complaint and little thanks from the beneficiaries. Claire had waited so long for the promised twelve thousand pounds that she had become an embittered and very disagreeable woman. She promptly invested the money unwisely and lost much of it, for which she blamed everyone but herself.

Hunt demanded his bequest in a lump sum instead of in the form of annual payments, which were all that the diminished estate could manage. He even brought a lawyer with him to Field Place to threaten a suit if his wish were not granted. Mary remained firm and, after a good deal of argument, the lawyer took his client away. As for Hogg, he wrote a humorously sharp-edged letter to Mary about her and her "baronet-boy" and their newly attained affluence.

In the spring of 1848 Percy brought an attractive young widow, Jane St. John, to call upon Mary with the announcement that they were engaged to be married. The girl described her future mother-in-law at the time of this meeting as "fair, lovely, almost girlish-looking, as slight as a reed with beautiful clear eyes. She put out her hand as she rose in greeting, saying, almost timidly, 'I'm Mary Shelley.' "

To Mary's delight Jane was already an admirer of Shelley's works and, after her marriage to Percy in June, she became Mary's staunchest ally in preserving and enhancing Shelley's memory. When they moved from the damp, unhealthy site of Field Place to a new home, Boscombe Manor, Jane turned one of the rooms into a veritable shrine, in which she gathered every bit of Shelley memorabilia which she could find.

Jane was also protectively devoted to Mary. When Claire arrived on one of her complaining and unwelcome visits to the Shelley household, Mary took her daughter-in-law aside. "Please don't leave me alone with her," she begged. "She has been the bane of my life ever since I was three years old." Jane complied and afterward managed to shield Mary permanently from Claire's sharp and nagging presence.

Sheltering love, comfort, and serenity! Was it possible that these three blessings had come at last to Mary Shelley? In 1850 she accompanied her son and his wife once again to Europe and wrote from Nice to a friend, "I never deserved so much peace and happiness as I enjoy with them." The only shadow now was that she always seemed to be tired, always so tired. On her return to her own house in Chester Square, London, she found herself content to sit quietly, for almost the first time in her life, neither reading, studying, nor writing. Instead, her thoughts ranged over her store of memories, picturing those she had known and loved the best. The mother she had never seen but had adored through her written words and her portrait; the father to whom her loyal heart had clung devotedly in spite of what her clear mind told her of his faults; Fanny, poor, poor Fanny; her three little lost children; and Shelley. *Shelley!*

How clearly she was seeing him during these quiet hours, a bright, immortal spirit, brave, ardent, and forever young! Was he actually drawing nearer to her now that her own life was gradually fading? Mary found herself smiling gently at the thought.

By the opening of the new year she had suffered a stroke from which she did not recover. She died on February 21, 1851, with Percy and Jane in loving attendance.

PRINCIPAL SOURCES

Armstrong, Margaret. *Trelawny: A Man's Life.* New York, Macmillan, 1940.

Biglund, Eileen. *Mary Shelley.* New York, Appleton-Century-Crofts, 1959.

George, Margaret. *One Woman's "Situation": A Study of Mary Wollstonecraft.* Urbana, Ill., University of Illinois Press, 1970.

Godwin, Mary Wollstonecraft. *A Vindication of the Rights of Women.* New York, W. W. Norton, 1967.

Marchand, Leslie A. *Byron: A Biography.* New York, Alfred A. Knopf, 1957.

Marshall, Mrs. Julian. *Life and Letters of Mary Wollstonecraft Shelley.* London, Richard Bentley, 1889.

Maurois, André. *Ariel: The Life of Shelley.* New York, Frederick Ungar, 1952.

Peck, Walter Edwin. *Shelley: His Life and Work.* Boston, Houghton Mifflin Company, 1927.

Smith, Elton Edward and Esther Greenwell. *William Godwin.* New York, Twayne Publishers, 1966.

Trelawny, Edward John. *The Last Days of Shelley and Byron.* New York, Doubleday Anchor Books, 1952.

White, Newman Ivey. *Shelley.* New York, Alfred A. Knopf, 1940.

Woolf, Virginia. *The Second Common Reader* (article on Mary Wollstonecraft). New York, Harcourt, Brace, 1932.

Original Letters in the Huntington Memorial Library, San Marino, California, from Mary Shelley to Leigh and Marianne Hunt, John Howard Payne, Sir John Browning, and Claire Clairmont, dated from 1817 through 1845.

INDEX

Adonais, 149, 150

Adventures of a Younger Son, The, 214

Aglietti, Dr., 114, 115

Alastor, or the Spirit of Solitude, 55, 58–9, 85

Alba, *see* Allegra

Albé, *see* Byron, Lord

Albion House, 86, 92–6, 98–100

Allegra, 91, 92, 95, 101, 104–7, 110–23, 117, 120, 132, 137, 149, 151, 153, 157, 158, 165–167, 170, 171; *see also* Elise *and* Shelley, Percy Bysshe

Ariosto, 109, 121

Bath, 79–80, 90–1

Baxter, Christie, 16, 17, 18

Baxter, Isabella, 16, 17, 19, 99, 109

Baxter, William, 15–20, 93, 96, 99

Bell, Dr., 126, 132, 133, 136

Bolivar, 177, 188, 190

Bonaparte, Napoleon, 12, 20, 37, 104

Booth, Mr., 99

Botji, Dr., and family, 141

Brunnen, 42–3

Burr, Aaron, 14

Byron, Lord, 47, 65, 66, 67, 70, 74, 116, 118, 119, 132, 160, 193, 205, 208, 216; and Claire, 57, 59, 64, 65, 71, 75–80, 104–6, 111, 157, 158, 165, 166, 170, 172, 208, 216; and Mary, 57, 63–70, 193, 195, 197–8, 206; and Shelley's work, 59–60; to Geneva, 60, 62–3; and Shelley, 63–71, 77–79, 91, 95, 104–6, 111–13, 116–17, 137, 149, 151–3, 158–9, 166, 170, 205, 206; and Wordsworth, 70–1; and Fanny, 72; letters to, from Shelley, 104, 105, 106, 137; in Venice, 104, 106, 110, 116–117; and Countess Guiccioli, 137, 149, 151, 152, 195; and Leigh Hunt, 154, 158–9, 181, 183–4, 193–6, 198; in Pisa, 154–70; and liberal periodical, 154, 159, 181, 184, 195–6; and boats, 163, 177, 178; and

Byron, Lord (*cont'd*)
The Examiner, 184; and Shelley accident, 186–8; at Shelley funeral, 191; as Shelley executor, 192–3; and Greek war, 196–8; death of, 195–6; *see also* Allegra; Hunt, Marianne; and *titles of works*

Caldéron, 127, 132, 162, 178
Casa Lanfranchi, 156, 157, 183–184, 186–7
Casa Magni, 172–3, 175, 180, 188–90
Casa Negroto, 193
Castle of Chillon, 70
Cenci, The, 125, 127, 130, 131, 138
Chamonix, 71
Childe Harold's Pilgrimage, 64–5, 71, 79, 112
Clairmont, Charles, 4, 12, 19, 21, 54–5, 98, 132, 192
Clairmont, Claire (Jane), 4, 5, 7–8, 12, 13, 17, 19, 20–1, 43–4, 46, 50, 56, 71, 89, 91, 103, 105, 106, 112, 119, 123, 125, 127, 139, 152, 179, 185, 186, 192, 200, 202, 208, 220, 222; and Aaron Burr, 14–15; changes name, 46; and Byron, 47, 57, 59, 64, 65, 71, 75–80, 104–6, 111, 157, 158, 165, 166, 170, 172, 208, 216; and Shelley, 47–9, 56, 61, 71, 89, 98, 141, 144, 166–7, 208, 221; and Mary and Shelley, 23, 28–9, 30, 32–43, 46–51, 59, 60, 79, 80, 81, 92, 95, 141, 145, 151,

169–70, 179; letter from Charles to, 54–5; pregnancy of, 75–6; and Fanny's death, 84; and Sophia Stacey, 134; in Florence, 141, 145, 157, 174, 175; and Emilia, 146–7; and Allegra's death, 171, 172, 174–5; and Trelawny, 213, 217; and Harrow, 215; *see also* Allegra; Byron, Lord; and Mason, Mrs.
Cogni, Margarita, 117
Coleridge, Samuel, 8, 9, 10, 72, 204
Cooper, James Fenimore, 204
Curran, Amelia, 126, 129

de Boinville, Mrs., 32
Del Rosso, Federigo, 138
Don Juan, 177–8, 187, 188
Drummond, Sir William, 124

Eldon, Lord, 91, 94, 96, 98
Elena Adelaide, 123, 140
Elise, 61, 79, 80, 81, 92, 106, 110–11, 117, 123, 152, 166
Epipsychidion, 146, 154–5
Este, 113, 117–18

Frankenstein, or the Modern Prometheus, 69, 71, 81, 96, 97–8, 100, 109–10, 138, 195, 200–201, 203
French Revolution, 80

Gamba, Count, 151, 157, 167–9, 195
Gamba, Pietro, 151, 157, 197
Gisborne, Maria and John, 107–109, 111–13, 126, 130, 138,

139, 140–1, 147–8, 151, 155, 203

Godwin and Co., 5, 7, 11

Godwin, Fanny, 3–8, 12, 13, 17, 19, 20, 21, 23, 26, 46, 51, 72–73, 81–4, 107, 108, 223

Godwin, William, 3–6, 9, 11, 12, 13–14, 17, 18, 19, 21, 22, 27, 28, 29, 31, 32, 45–6, 52, 56, 58, 59, 60, 73, 81, 82, 83–4, 88–9, 90, 93, 97, 98, 100, 107, 108, 119, 131–2, 135, 167, 194–5, 201, 204, 216, 218; *see also* Godwin and Co.; Godwin, Mrs. William; Shelley, Mary Godwin, and her father

Godwin, Mrs. William, 4–8, 9, 11, 12, 13, 15, 17, 18, 19, 20, 21, 22–3, 24, 28, 29, 30, 31, 35–6, 38, 46, 56, 82, 83, 200, 201, 218; *see also* Godwin and Co.; Godwin, William; and Shelley, Mary Godwin, and her stepmother

Godwin, William Jr., 4, 5, 12, 13, 14, 19, 21, 200, 201

Great Marlow, 86, 97

Greeks, and war of independence, 147, 148, 156, 196–7

Gregson, 215

Guiccioli, Teresa, 137, 149, 151, 152, 153, 157, 167, 168, 186, 193, 195, 206, 209

Guilford, Lord, 124

Harris, Henry, 130, 131

Hate, 41

Hay, Captain, 167–8

Haydon, Benjamin, 92

Hazlitt, Henry, 92, 204

Hellas, 156

Hercules, 197, 198

"Hermit of Marlow, The," 97

Hogg, Thomas Jefferson, 48–50, 55, 98, 100, 193, 207, 208, 209, 221

Hookham, 38, 86–7

Hoppner, R. B., and family, 106, 111, 112, 116, 120, 132, 137, 152, 166

Hôtel de Vienne, 37

Hunt, Leigh, 85–6, 87, 91, 92, 93, 98, 99, 100, 101, 103, 129, 130–1, 132, 138, 154, 156–7, 159, 180, 181, 183–4, 191, 192, 195–6, 199, 208, 221

Hunt, Marianne, 91, 99, 129, 146, 154, 157, 165, 183, 184, 193–4, 199, 206

Hunt, Thornton, 93–4

Hymn to Intellectual Beauty, 70, 91

Imlay, Gilbert, 82

Indian Serenade, 134

"Influence of Government on the Character of the People," 14

Institution for the Formation of Character, 72–3

Journal of a Six Weeks Tour, 98

Julian and Maddalo, 118

Keats, John, 85, 86, 92, 100, 140, 149, 178

Kenney, John, 199

Kubla Khan, 72

Lackington and Hughes (publishers), 100
Lake Como, 105
Lake Leman, 69–70, 73, 116
Lamb, Charles, 7, 9, 15, 72, 100, 103, 129, 203
Lamb, Mary, 7, 100, 203
Lancetta, 178, 187
Laon and Cythna, 97
Last Man, The, 105, 207–8, 216
Leghorn, 107–8, 127, 129–30, 138–9, 180–3
Leigh, Augusta, 111
Lerici, 173–4, 186
Lewis, M. G., 74–5
Liberal, The, 195–6
Life of Lord Byron, 209
Lines Written Among the Euganean Hills, 118, 120
Lodore, 216
Lucca, 109
Lyons, 103

Maglian, Signor, 173, 186
Maison Chapuis, 66, 71, 220
"Manchester Massacre," 130
Manfred, 79
Marriage of Figaro, The, 100
Masi, 167–9
Mask of Anarchy, The, 130–1
Mason, Mrs., 132–3, 136, 137, 138, 141, 144, 145
Mason, Mr., 165–6
Mavrokordatos, Prince, 147–8, 156
Mazeppa, 117
Medwin, Tom, 142–4, 148, 149, 159, 160, 164, 206
Memoirs of Lord Byron, 206

Milan, 104–5
Milly, 92, 113
Mocenigo Palace, 106, 116–17
Monk, The, 74
Moore, Thomas, 15, 66, 209, 210–11
Murray, John, 81, 96

Naples, 120–2
Necessity for Atheism, The, 22, 48
Nightmare Abbey, 128
Nott, Reverend Dr., 159–60
Novello, Mary, 203–4

Ode to Naples, 140
Ode to a Skylark, 139
Ode to Venice, 117
Ode to the West Wind, 133
Ollier (publishers), 96, 97, 98, 99, 133, 144, 149, 156, 167
Othello, 164
Owen, Robert, 72–3

Pacchiani, Francesco, 145, 146, 147
Palazzo Galetti, 144
Palazzo Marini, 133
Paolo, 110, 111, 114, 123, 138–139, 152
Paris, 37–9, 199–200, 212
Payne, John Howard, 200, 207
Peacock, Thomas Love, 42, 48, 53–4, 55, 71, 80, 85, 93, 97, 99, 100, 118, 125, 128, 130, 131, 192, 195
Petman, Miss, 12–13
Pisa, 107, 132, 137, 139, 143–150, 156–72, 186, 190

Pistol Club, 158, 167
Plato, 109, 178
Pliny, 105
Polidori, Dr., 63, 64, 66–7, 74
Political Justice, 22, 23
Pope, Dr., 55–6
Pósthumous Poems, 204–5
Prisoner of Chillon, 70, 79
Prometheus, 104
Prometheus Unbound, 104, 118, 124, 125, 133, 138
Proposal for Putting Reform to the Vote, etc., 97

Queen Mab, 22, 27, 59

Rambles in Germany and Italy, 220
Ravenna, 151–4
Reform Bill, 217
Reveley, Henry, 107, 108, 135, 140, 149–50
Reveley, Mrs., 107
Revolt of Islam, The, 97, 99, 142
Richard the Lion-Hearted, 80
Rime of the Ancient Mariner, 8–9, 204
Roberts, Captain, 160, 163, 187, 188
Rome, 121, 124–7
Rosalind and Helen, 109, 129
Rouen, 80
Rousseau, Jean-Jacques, 70, 103

St. John, Jane, 221–2
San Terenzo, 172, 173, 175–6, 188
Sécheron, 61–6

Sgricci, Tomaso, 145
Shakespeare, William, 42, 43, 56, 128
Shelley, Sir Bysshe, 24, 49, 52
Shelley, Charles, 47, 86, 88, 89, 94, 96, 100, 193, 208
Shelley, Clara Everina, 98, 99, 101, 110, 112–15, 116, 119–120, 121, 178, 180
Shelley, Harriet, 18, 25, 26, 29–30, 32, 40–1, 44–5, 47, 48, 52, 87, 180; *see also* Shelley, Mary Godwin, *and* Shelley, Percy Bysshe, and first wife
Shelley, Ianthe, 25, 26, 40, 86, 88, 89, 94, 96, 100
Shelley, John, 220
Shelley, Mary Godwin, and her mother, 3–4, 6–7, 107–8, 130, 145, 179, 223; and her father, 3, 4, 5, 12, 13, 14, 16, 20, 23, 24, 28, 31, 45–6, 48, 49, 58, 73, 83–4, 88–9, 93, 96, 107, 108, 119, 131, 135, 137, 139, 167, 194, 200–2, 216, 217, 223; and her stepmother, 4, 5, 7, 11, 15, 58, 96, 137, 200, 218; education of, 4, 14; and Southey, 8; and Coleridge, 8–10; illness of, 11–12, 13, 15–16, 209, 211, 216; at Ramsgate, 12–13; writings of, 14, 41, 42, 69, 81, 96, 98, 105, 118, 138, 140, 150, 194, 195, 205, 206, 207, 216, 220; *see also titles of works*; and Aaron Burr, 14–15; at Dundee, 16–17, 18–20; early relations with

Shelley, Mary Godwin (cont'd)
Shelley, 21–5, 26–8, 30–3;
and Harriet Shelley, 29–30,
32, 40–1, 180, 218; elopes
with Shelley, 32–3; journal of,
34, 37, 43, 44, 47, 51, 71, 91,
121, 136, 143, 192, 204, 206,
210, 211, 214–18; in Paris,
37–9, 199–200, 212; to Switzerland, 39–43; studies Greek,
46, 47, 48, 55, 81, 147; preg-
nancies of, 47, 48, 49, 50, 55–
58, 94, 98, 126, 128, 133, 167,
178, 179; and Claire's pregnancy, 76–7; depression of, 80,
85, 99, 119–21, 124, 128,
165, 175, 178, 209–10; studies
Latin, 81; takes up drawing
and painting, 81, 125, 158;
and Fanny, 82–4; marries Shelley, 88–9; and Albion House,
94–6; letters to Shelley, 99;
and Byron's palace, 117; and
Byron's ms., 117, 118; and
Elise, 123–4; see also Elise;
and son Percy, 133, 173, 175,
176, 178, 180, 183, 191, 210,
219, 220; and Sophia Stacey,
134; and Keats, 140; and Emilia, 146–7, 155; and Dr. Nott,
160; and Allegra's death, 171,
173, 175; and Shelley's fatal
trip, 180–3, 185, 186–9; and
Shelley's death, 192–3; financial situation of, 192, 195,
196, 197–8, 201, 202, 208,
214, 215, 216; letter to Hunts,
201; and Shelley biography,
201, 206, 213, 215, 220, 221;
and Shelley poems, 202, 204,
205, 209, 215, 218–19; suitors
of, 207, 213; and Byron biography, 209; and Trelawny autobiography, 213–14; and Trelawny's daughter, 217; death
of, 223

Shelley, Percy Bysshe, 18, 21–5,
26–7, 42, 43–4, 45, 47, 56,
58, 59–60, 66, 67–8, 71–2,
74–5, 92, 97, 103, 112–14,
120–2, 135, 138, 140–1, 144–
145, 151, 152, 154, 159, 164,
167–8, 178, 179, 180, 198;
and first wife, 18, 25, 26, 40–
41; see also Shelley, Harriet;
trysts with Mary, 23–5; 26,
32, 45; and laudanum, 25, 30,
31; financial problems of, 38,
42–6, 49–50, 52, 74, 79, 98,
100, 135; illness of, 40–1, 52–
53, 54, 99, 113, 114, 122, 124,
132–3, 136, 139, 140, 150;
writing by, 41, 42, 55, 70, 97,
104, 109, 118, 122–5, 127,
130, 133, 134, 139, 140, 146,
149, 150, 154–5; see also titles
of works; and Wordsworth, 45,
70–1; death of grandfather,
49–50; letter to Godwin, 60;
and Claire's pregnancy, 76–7;
and Byron mss., 79, 80–1, 112;
and Keats, 86, 100, 140, 149;
and custody of children, 87–8,
90, 91, 94; and Allegra, 91,
95, 104–6, 111–12, 117, 137,
149, 151, 153, 171, 175; and

adoption of child, 123, 140; studies Spanish, 127, 132; and Caldéron, 127–8, 132, 162; and Sophia Stacey, 134; and Medwin, 143, 144; and Emilia, 146–7, 151, 154–5; and boats, 149–50, 162–3, 175–8; and liberal periodical, 154, 159, 181, 184; and Greek war, 156; and swimming, 163–4, 176; fatal trip of, 180–2, 185–9; funeral service for, 190–1; memorial to, 196–7; work of, in England, 201, 220; will of, 208, 221; see also Godwin, Fanny; Godwin, Mrs. William; Clairmont, Claire; Byron, Lord; Trelawny, Edward

Shelley, Percy F., 133, 141, 151, 165, 172, 173, 175, 176, 180, 183, 191, 193, 194, 198, 199, 200, 206, 210, 215–26; see also Shelley, Sir Timothy

Shelley, Sir Timothy, 24–5, 89, 103, 159, 193, 195, 196, 201, 204–5, 206, 208, 209, 213, 215, 220

Shelley, William, 58, 60, 61, 79, 80, 81, 96, 98, 99, 101, 110, 113, 118, 119, 125, 126–7, 131, 178, 180, 191

Smith, Horace, and family, 92, 93, 100, 199

Southey, Robert, 6, 8, 10, 58

Spezia, 172

Stacey, Sophia, 134–5

Stanzas Written in Dejection Near Naples, 122

Susa, 104

Swellfoot, 140

Symposium, 109

Taafe, John, 147, 167–8

Tasso, 109, 121

Trelawny, Edward John, 143, 148, 160–4, 167–8, 172, 173, 174, 176–7, 187–91, 193, 201, 210, 213–14

Vacca, Dr., 136, 183

Vagabond, The, 93

Valperga, 118, 138, 140, 150, 156, 167, 201

Venice, 104, 106, 110, 114, 116, 117, 120

Villa Cappucini, 112, 117

Villa Deodati, 66, 220

Villa Pliniana, 105, 107

Villa Valsovano, 127

Vindication of the Rights of Women, The, 4, 23

Vision of Judgement, The, 184

Vivian, Charles, 177, 178, 189

Viviani, Emilia, 145–7, 151, 154

Voltaire, 70, 103

Westbrooks, 87–8, 90, 91

Whitton, 196, 201, 205, 215

William IV, coronation of, 214–215

Williams, Edward Eleker, 143, 148, 149–50, 154, 156, 158–161, 162–3, 164, 169, 170, 174, 175–8, 182, 185–9, 190–191

Williams, Edward Jr., 148

Williams, Helen, 37, 38

Williams, Jane, 148, 157–8, 161–165, 170, 178, 180–1, 185–9, 192–3, 207, 210–11

Williams, Rosalind, 148

Witch of Atlas, The, 140

Wollstonecraft, Mary, 3, 4, 5, 6–7, 17, 20, 21, 23, 47, 59, 73, 97, 107–8, 130, 132, 145, 217; *see also* Shelley, Mary Godwin, and her mother

Wordsworth, William, 45, 70–1